D0777319

DON'T JUST SIT THERE!

DON'T JUST SIT THERE!

44 INSIGHTS TO GET YOUR MEDITATION PRACTICE OFF THE CUSHION AND INTO THE REAL WORLD

BIET SIMKIN

ENLIVEN BOOKS

—

ATRIA

NEW YORK   LONDON   TORONTO   SYDNEY   NEW DELHI

ENLIVEN
ATRIA

An Imprint of Simon & Schuster, Inc.
1230 Avenue of the Americas
New York, NY 10020

First Enliven Books hardcover edition April 2019

ENLIVEN BOOKS / ATRIA BOOKS and colophon are trademarks of Simon & Schuster, Inc.

For information about special discounts for bulk purchases, please contact Simon & Schuster Special Sales at 1-866-506-1949 or business@simonandschuster.com.

The Simon & Schuster Speakers Bureau can bring authors to your live event. For more information or to book an event, contact the Simon & Schuster Speakers Bureau at 1-866-248-3049 or visit our website at www.simonspeakers.com.

Interior design by Kyoko Watanabe

Manufactured in the United States of America

10 9 8 7 6 5 4 3 2 1

Library of Congress Cataloging-in-Publication Data

Names: Simkin, Biet, author.
Title: Don't just sit there! : 44 insights to get your meditation practice off the cushion and into the real world / Biet Simkin.
Description: New York : Atria/Enliven Books, 2019.
Identifiers: LCCN 2018038292 (print) | LCCN 2018052040 (ebook) | ISBN 9781501193217 (eBook) | ISBN 9781501193194 (hardback) | ISBN 9781501193200 (paperback)
Subjects: LCSH: Self-actualization (Psychology) | Meditation. | Mind and body. | BISAC: BODY, MIND & SPIRIT / Meditation. | SELF-HELP / Meditations. | SELF-HELP / Personal Growth / Happiness.
Classification: LCC BF637.S4 (ebook) | LCC BF637.S4 S5484 2019 (print) | DDC 158.1/2—dc23
LC record available at https://urldefense.proofpoint.com/v2/url?u=https-3A__lccn.loc.gov
_2018038292&d=DwIFAg&c=jGUuvAdBXp_VqQ6t0yah2g&r=CKb5CuAEzBQ_Amr8XCMf4b
Xh9SWvuO6mXnu4MO7oDRChWClhgwpp1zLgHYux9qXV&m=bvxWCCbBOns6ygM8L9EU
3QG9TB-O0qZfmaaz6KUZ-ss&s=hdmC8bZDZEieGrUOiZSu6UxDrfYaLVRNdPcc3bTrPf4&e=

ISBN 978-1-5011-9319-4
ISBN 978-1-5011-9321-7 (ebook)

Dear Papa,

Do you remember the morning I crawled around the kitchen floor on an acid trip? You walked in with a big grin on your face and said, in your heavy Russian accent, "Guess where I have been all night?" I looked up in an acid-washed state of wonder and asked, "Where?" "Well, prison," you replied. "Yes, they found my fake driver's license, and I spent the night in a jail cell."

You looked so happy, like you just won the Lotto, and that's just how you approached every single fucking moment, even the worst ones. "Now, I go to take a nap," you said, and ambled to your bedroom. Lying on the floor, I realized I wasn't enlightened like you, even with all those chemicals designed to expand my mind. In that moment, I knew I wanted to learn everything you could teach me. You didn't make it to see me write this book, but I want you to know I figured it out.

This book is for you.

I love you,
Bietinka

CONTENTS

Introduction   1

Forrest Gump Is the Soul   7

Meditation 101   11

1. The Law of Divided Attention   15

2. The Law of Aim   20

3. The Law of Identification   25

4. The Law of Shocks   30

5. The Law of Three   34

6. The Law of Self-Remembering   39

7. The Law of Personality   44

8. The Law of Equals   48

9. The Law of Seven (Law of Success)   52

10. The Law of Super Efforts   58

11. The Law of "Shoulds"   62

12. The Law of Mechanical Goodness   66

13. The Law of Negative Emotions   70

14. The Law of Buffers   75

15. The Law of Leaks   79

16. The Law of Inner Considering   83

17. The Law of Householding   87

18. The Law of the ABCs of Influence   92

19. The Law of Accident   97

20. The Law of Self-Will   101

21. The Law of Sex Energy   105

22. The Law of the Six Processes of Love   109

23. The Law of Desire   113

24. The Law of Payment   117

25. The Law of Knowledge, Being, and Understanding   122

26. The Law of Conscious Suffering   126

27. The Law of Human Types   131

28. The Law of Chief Features   137

29. The Law of Accumulators   142

30. The Law of Unnecessary Talk   146

31. The Law of Lying   150

32. The Law of Recurrence   154

33. The Law of Death   158

34. The Law of Three Wishes   163

35. The Law of Imagination   167

36. The Law of the Four Centers   171

37. The Law of Imposters   176

38. The Law of Pain   180

39. The Law of Duality   185

40. The Law of the Body   190

41. The Law of Beholding   194

42. The Law of Opening   199

43. The Law of Focus   203

44. The Law of Crystallization   207

You and I, We Wrote This Book   211

Acknowledgments   213

Resources   219

DON'T JUST SIT THERE!

INTRODUCTION

I learned to meditate in diapers. Two years old, and my shaman father (think Mr. Miyagi meets Santa Claus), lifted my nearly naked baby body into his Zenned-out home office to breathe deeply, meditate, and climb into lotus pose. Next to tall stacks of texts—Rumi, Alan Watts, Jung—I planted tiny headstands, gazed into his hazel eyes, and listened as he spoke about love, the soul, and humanity's common purpose on this planet.

Conceived as a kind of freedom child in St. Petersburg by my Russian parents—who fled to Jackson Heights, Queens, to escape Soviet religious persecution—I was ready for the idyllic, all-American childhood I had come to see as my birthright by the time I was six. Then my mom was diagnosed with a terminal illness. Tragic. Sudden. Cancer. Within six months, she was gone. When asked to describe my childhood after that, I usually mention *Running with Scissors*, a memoir of a comically dysfunctional household headed by an eccentric therapist. If that doesn't do the trick, I tell them this story.

My father, a medical doctor by training, cured himself of tuberculosis with a shaman in the woods outside St. Petersburg via Ayurvedic medicine, yoga, and meditation. As the Soviets had banned these healing arts, my father saw America as the spot to establish a psychotherapeutic practice that integrated shamanic, spiritual traditions. Setting up his office in our new apartment, his clients tended to be, shall we say, eccentric. Once, as a teenager, I heard Bach's Goldberg Variations emanate from the living room, and strolled out of my bedroom to find his client—a pale woman in her twenties, bandaged wrists, shaved head— delicately pushing keys on our grand piano. One guy used to pee on our houseplants because he thought his urine was sacred!

A freethinker with a big gray beard and the kindest eyes, my father used to say that my shitty neighborhood public school was "conformist," that the teachers and students were "asleep." So I skipped classes to spend time alone in the library, reading Freud, Jung, and the other authors he favored. Nights and weekends, we meditated hours on end, and he trained me, after a fashion, in his psychotherapeutic and shamanic traditions. He also strutted around our apartment in his undies, played a mean saxophone, and drank me under the table. It was, shall we say, an unconventional childhood. And that's before I bring up my Mohawk-coiffed, metal head big brother. Hi, Genia!

Signed to a Sony recording contract at the tender age of twenty, my life blurred into a stream of limousines, recording studios, cocaine, heroin, and sex. After my mother's death, I felt like a window to my soul had cracked open, revealing a light that I desperately wanted to access. But I was stuck. Every once in a while when I was sober, I tried to meditate with my father like I used to, but it usually made the pain worse. It probably didn't help that I was the kind of "spiritual" person who took breaks in the middle of a yoga class to blow coke lines in the bathroom!

Dropped by Sony, my downward descent spiraled into chaos. I moved in with a guy more akin to a drug dealer than a partner, and lived in a world of fashion shows, nightclubs, and parties. Accidentally pregnant, I finally stayed sober, until my four-month-old daughter, Ula, died of SIDS. Half our apartment burned down, and we lived in the not burned out part for four months waiting for renovations. My best friend hung himself. None of this stopped me, but when my father died suddenly two years later, I cracked open completely. After a drug-fueled, hazy year straight out of *Requiem for a Dream*, I finally got sober.

When I finally kicked heroin, I committed to learn everything my father had tried to teach me while he was alive. I took stock of my messy life, disgusted by what I saw. At the time, I had no intention of writing a book; I was just searching for that *X-Files* truth. You know, the one that's out there. But the more I studied and applied what I learned to everyday experiences, I began to grasp the power of meditation as a tool for healing and break-through. At last, I realized the "out there" truth I had spent my entire life looking for was actually in *here*, deep down inside me.

My father used to say, "meditation and yoga are wonderful tools, but they're not the point." It didn't matter if I could medi-tate like a champ or pop up a kick-ass headstand; what mattered was that I could connect to my soul, and how awake I was to my true purpose on the planet. That required something new, and in mastering the spiritual toolkit I gleaned from my father, I now have access to an incredible spiritual high every day sans booze or blow.

I will be brutally honest: the work I teach isn't easy. Even as a precocious student, to transform in the way I craved required years of dedicated study. Sure, a meditative mind calms, but a serious practice typically kicks up a lot of unpleasant shit. It forces us to confront aspects of ourselves we may see as ugly or shameful. We may run right into reality when we'd rather blast off to fantasyland. Meditation is first about clarifying who you truly *are*. Only then can you begin to create who you want to *be*.

Many of the concepts and ideas I lay out in this book build

on a philosophy of enlightenment known as The Fourth Way, developed in the early twentieth century by the Greek-Armenian mystic and philosopher George Gurdjieff. The other three paths to spiritual enlightenment take the way of the yogi, the monk, and the fakir—ascetics who shed worldly aims to purify their souls. This Fourth Way shows that we don't have to escape modern life to reach enlightenment. Instead, you can use everyday experiences—a trip to the grocery store, a phone call with mom, the morning commute—to learn truths, practice mindfulness, and live on the spiritual plane. I like to think of this Fourth Way as a kind of "enlightenment for the rest of us."

You can visualize this practice as an effort to live at the intersection of two lines that form a cross.

Along the horizontal line run the tangible, external realities we face in the physical world. Kids. Cars. Conference calls. The vertical line, by contrast, is the invisible, spiritual dimension of reality—the world of meditation, prayer, and the soul. The monk and yogi live almost entirely on the vertical line, for example, while most of us live our lives on the horizontal. This Fourth Way shows us that *at the intersection of these lines* we can live materially satisfying cosmopolitan lives *and* satisfy our souls with transcendent spiritual bliss.

This philosophy teaches that all humans live under a set of spiritual laws that govern our experiences along the vertical and horizontal lines. These laws exert influence whether we're aware of them or not, and if we're inattentive, they can shape the contours of our lives in unpleasant ways. When I work with clients, I help them identify the laws working against them, then teach them how to integrate this knowledge into purposeful meditative practice. The process is messy, profound, and often a little painful. Over time, I've refined 44 of these laws as the backbone of my personal spiritual practice, as well as the work I do with my clients.

Since I acquired the tools to live above these laws, my life has transformed. No lie: when I started this work, I lived on food stamps and slept on friends' couches. Several years later, I lead meditations from L.A. to the Mediterranean coast and points beyond. I've built a thriving practice doing work I love. I interact with the state of gratitude in a way I never thought possible. I'm married to the man of my dreams. I could go on. And on. But it's not just me. I've helped clients overcome addiction, lose weight, trade unfulfilling jobs for dream careers and soul-sucking relationships for true love, embrace sexuality, and transform their lives in ways they could not possibly have imagined.

After I show you that the easiest way to understand your soul is to watch *Forrest Gump*, then share easy-to-use tools to meditate, the bite-sized chapters that follow lay out tiny, potent doses of spiritual info to walk you through steps you can take to live above the laws that keep you asleep on this planet. You'll begin with a meditative practice, building up to thirty minutes daily. As your practice unfolds, each law reveals itself chapter by chapter until you begin to grasp the key role it plays. Finally, for every law

I've designed an aligned exercise—a verification point—that will let you see the ways a law operates in your life, and show you how to live above it. I suggest you buy a nice new journal, as several of the verifications use written exercises. You can also use a journal to jot down new ideas and discoveries as you work through the laws.

Once you make the commitment to do this work, extraordinary things *will* happen. You have a choice, though. If you want to feel really, really good for three days, read this book all the way through. If you want to transform your life, then you'll need to meditate and do the exercises in each chapter, perhaps forming a study group to work through the laws with friends. The choice is yours. Really, no judgment. Either way, you win! But, these practices are the metaphysical equivalent of gym weights. When you lift, you chisel and tone your body. When you use these practices, you cut away the spiritual fat around your soul, sculpting your being into the masterpiece it was designed to be. As the process unfolds, you may realize you actually *are* your soul, and then you will find that anything . . . yes, *anything* . . . is possible.

At this point, you might ask, "What do you mean, I *am* my *soul*?" Well, to answer that question, we need to talk about Gump. Forrest Gump.

FORREST GUMP IS THE SOUL

Have you ever wondered what your soul looks like? Well, it looks a lot like Forrest Gump. No, your soul doesn't look like Tom Hanks! But Forrest's essence is the way your soul looks. As it turns out, sometimes in the inner world of a story you can find real, deep spiritual truths. I often use films, fairy tales, and parables like Harry Potter, Snow White, or Goldilocks with clients to illuminate a point or unravel hidden meanings. So it makes sense that up late one night watching *Forrest Gump* on TV, I realized it was similar to all the parables and fairy tales I had been decoding. In fact, I realized it was a story about the soul.

Okay, so how is Forrest the soul? Well, the soul is lucky, open to strange miracles, and "stupid" in a sense, because it doesn't *think* about anything at all! It's innocent, generous, and always forgives. In other words, the soul is a lot like Gump. It's a state of pure love, and it's the real *you*. A soul sits in a body, so you think you're a separate entity, but really the soul connects you to me via energy we can't see. Some call that energy God, the Universe, or the Divine. Labels matter little to the soul.

You *think* you're the body and mind, but you're not. They can be pathways to you, or blocks to the real you. It depends on how you use them. But no matter how you use them, they'll never be *you.* In fact, the mind and body tend to reject the soul. Lieutenant Dan and Jenny, Forrest's friends in the film, represent parts of the mind and body that rebel. To the mind, the soul is too innocent, too naive to "the ways of the world" to succeed. It's wrong.

Here on earth, though, where you don't use it a lot, the soul looks like a limp muscle, scrawny and weak. A mentally weak boy, Forrest walks awkwardly, too, with polio-induced leg braces. His schoolmates tease him. No surprise there, as a mind often mocks a soul's innocence. But one day, as he runs from bullies, his braces fall off, and he sprints away like a world champ. Teased mercilessly, Forrest finds out he runs really, really fast. To the soul, difficulty is a gift that wakes you up to your powers. As you meditate to face difficulty, I can't wait to hear what powers you wake up!

A gentle innocent, the soul can't see spite and always forgives. Lieutenant Dan calls Forrest an "imbecile," but he doesn't notice the insult, and smiles. Jenny spits nasty words at him, but Forrest responds only with love. Depicted as "slow" or stupid, Forrest actually operates on a level above insults. His "slowness" isn't an impairment; it's an asset. Via meditation, you can slow down to the same kind of soul time, dissolve anger, and forgive the slings and arrows that come at you in life.

A part of you seeks the soul, but like Jenny, looks in all the wrong places. As an innocent child, she sees the soul and befriends Forrest. But as an adult, she forgets where she found the soul's bliss. It's like an itch she can't scratch, so she destroys herself trying to find it again in cocaine and casual sex, the pleasures of the body. Instead, she finds hepatitis C. Forrest, the soul, shows up in her life over and over, but she rejects him. The soul is not sexy and glamorous enough for Jenny. Still, her dark journey is a necessary one. If we did not get lost, how would we be found?

So many of us are like Jenny, looking for a soul mate. Here's the big irony, though: *your soul is your soul mate*. It's what you're looking for. I sought my soul in heroin, whiskey, and dates with anorexic models I thought might be "the one." Some seek souls in careers, cash, or activist causes. It doesn't matter. Without a link to your true self, none of it works the way you want. On the flip side, once you make the soul your mate, and make *all* other relationships secondary, problems fade and miracles appear.

Forrest, the soul, is always open to miracles, magic, and kismet. Elvis happens to stay at his mom's bed and breakfast, so Forrest teaches him to dance. He accidentally runs across a football field one day, so he gets to be an All-American football player and go to college for free. Forrest accidentally starts a multimillion-dollar company. He invests in a new computer company called Apple. When you open to your soul, you open yourself to a life of miracles and magic.

Our minds tend to reject the magic of the soul, like Lieutenant Dan. He thinks he knows exactly how life is supposed to go. He has a plan. When life goes off script, he rages at life, Forrest, and God. Dan wants to die in battle with his men, like his father. Wounded in the jungle, he yells, "Leave me here," but Forrest saves him. After he loses his legs, he screams at Forrest, "I had a destiny . . . now I'm nothing but a goddamn cripple, a legless freak!" His make-believe destiny lost, Dan thinks his life is over.

Like many of us, Lieutenant Dan can't accept what *is*. Suicidal over the loss of his legs, he tries to drink himself to death in his wheelchair. What he doesn't know yet is he'll be reborn, in a sense, with a wife, a Fortune 500 company, and titanium legs. At some point, we too must have a dream or plan go terribly wrong. The ability to know at times our plans and ideas are wrong is key to living a conscious life. So, pause and ask yourself, "How do I respond when life doesn't work out the way I want?"

It is quite funny and a great tragedy, but most of us have to die before we become willing to *be* with the soul. When we return to be with it, though, the soul is so happy to see us! Over and over again in the film, Forrest, the soul, asks to be with Jenny. But it's only when she's dying that Jenny finally surrenders to the soul, and asks Forrest to marry her. He says yes, of course. The mind tries on no and maybe, but the soul always says yes.

You don't have to wait till you're dying to reunite with your soul, though. In fact, this little book is meant to teach you how to choose your soul, again and again, even as you live a modern, fast-paced life. You're so afraid if you surrender to your soul, you'll be lonely, weird, or rejected, an alien to the world. Who wants to be like that? Nobody! But that's just a trick. The truth is, when you get to know your soul, you'll still have your personality: the moxie and sexiness of Jenny, say, or the courage and business acumen of Lieutenant Dan. But you'll also get access to the miracles, vulnerability, and sweetness of the soul. You'll wear your personality like an outfit, but it will reveal the real you.

◇◇◇◇◇◇◇◇◇◇◇◇◇◇◇◇◇◇◇◇◇◇◇◇◇◇
You'll wear your personality like an outfit, but it will reveal the real you.
◇◇◇◇◇◇◇◇◇◇◇◇◇◇◇◇◇◇◇◇◇◇◇◇◇◇

Verification Point

After you've read this chapter, go watch the film, viewing it through the lens of the soul. Use questions to shape your experience as you watch. In what ways has the story of your soul been similar to Forrest's? Are you seeking like Jenny? Are you in rebellion like Lieutenant Dan? Look for areas in your life where you may reject the soul, as well as areas where you embrace it.

MEDITATION 101

Meditation. It sounds so serious, even intimidating. Maybe the word conjures up an image of a yogi with a long beard on top of a mountain, or a monk living in silence. But meditation isn't just for those guys. It's for you, too. Often a playful, joyous experience, meditation also requires patience, persistence, and practice. So why should you put in the energy to cultivate a meditative lifestyle? Well, it might just be the best gift you can possibly give yourself. Sit in a conscious state using tools and techniques I teach, and you may just become the best version of yourself you can imagine. But don't *just* sit there. Meditation travels well, and its real impact kicks in when you walk out the door.

There's no one right way to meditate, but I've found a few moves make sense. First, find a space where you can sit comfortably, without interruption, and especially if you're new to meditation, make it *beautiful.* Light candles, listen to soothing music, or gaze at a lovely piece of art or a bouquet of freshly cut flowers. Begin with your eyes open and focus on a lit candle or point in the room (anything works; there's no need to get precious about it). Focus your gaze as you inhale deeply through the nose; pull the breath deeply into your belly for a few seconds, and release.

Ideally, sit and meditate for thirty minutes when you wake up, though if you need a cup of coffee first or a shower to get your blood flowing, go for it! The point is that you do it. If you're new to the practice, or find you can't handle a full thirty minutes just yet, start with a shorter time period, say ten or fifteen minutes, and gradually increase the minutes until you reach thirty. Regardless of how long you meditate, you need to commit to doing so at least five days a week. This is nonnegotiable. As with any skill—speaking French, running for distance—meditation requires consistent practice. If you don't feel "good" at meditation at first, you're not alone. I bet you can't pick up a cello and play Bach's Cello Suites without practice, either. So don't fret. *Practice.*

If you find your mind wandering, don't worry about it. You can bring your attention back to your breath and the focal point you've chosen, or just let the thoughts come and go. They're going to pass, and then there will be new ones. No big deal. The point is stay in the meditation. Feel free to focus on the feeling of your sit bones grounding you to your seat, a mantra you may have been given, and the sounds or music filling the room around you. The goal here is to reach a certain state, a kind of blissed-out neutrality that turns down the volume on your thoughts and fosters clarity.

Meditation opens a link to your interior world, and to access this space, you need to both listen and speak. You meditate to listen, so also speak via a tactic I like to call asking or what most people call prayer. In the morning and during your day, talk to this universal energy that powers your soul. You can whisper asks like, "please give me clarity of purpose," or, "power me with the energy I need to create joy today." Ask to be free from worry and anger, or ask to be shown true love. In making these petitions, you make yourself available to receive and expand. So, go ahead. Go get power beyond measure.

I read somewhere that if you don't ask, the answer is always no. In other words, the universe won't intervene in your life until you ask for help. But for many of us, prayer can be a bit of a loaded term, so I developed the concept of asking. Asking is a way to talk to your soul. Without this tool, you live a life of body and mind only, which is a little dull, don't you think? So, cultivate a willingness to ask for divine help. Use this tool to ask for guidance and strength. Or, just strike up a conversation with your new invisible Friend. It really works!

If you'd like, you can also use breath work to supplement your meditation practice. Sitting cross-legged, breathe deeply in and out through the nose. As you inhale, lean back, and splay your shoulders like angel wings. As you exhale, lean forward, curving your back a bit. Do this for fifteen minutes once a week or so, breathing deeply and gently repeating the motion. It's a simple technique, but used often, this practice will make you conscious of your breathing, an essential prerequisite for a meditative practice.

Listening to spiritual music helps, too. My record *The Lunar* was designed to augment a meditative breathing practice, so feel free to listen to it as you breathe and meditate!

Before I devoted my life to a meditative practice and cultivated a relationship with my soul, I often felt alone and insecure. Today, I like to drive my life with a copilot, my soul. It is the primary relationship in my life, with me through thick and thin, in moments of sorrow and triumph. While our thoughts, emotions, and bodies betray us at some point or other, the soul remains consistent, neutral, above it all. As you begin to unpack the 44 Laws of the Universe you've lived under for nearly your entire life,

I urge you to use meditation to strengthen your connection to the soul. It's the only mechanism that can generate the kind of power you need to live above these laws and fulfill your true purpose. So, what are these laws that keep you from enlightenment? Let's find out.

1

THE LAW OF DIVIDED ATTENTION

Perhaps you've noticed it in your own life: at moments in morning meditation, you're cool as a cucumber. Calm. Composed. Carefree. You sit on a cushion, perhaps next to a few candles, and sense clarity, ease, and stillness. The rest of the time, though, it's a different story. You're neurotic and busy; you freak out and worry. The tools you test in the morning simply don't translate to the rest of the day. If you recognize this split, you're not alone!

So often, meditation presents only as a sanctuary, or a retreat from the stresses of modern life. No doubt, it can be. But its real work is to shine the inner light you cultivate in stillness out into the everyday. How do you go about this? Well, you need a set of tools to use when you're off the cushion, too. Happily, you possess this toolkit already. It's in your being. You possess the power to pause, float above yourself, and stilly observe

> You possess the power to pause, float above yourself, and stilly observe as you work, play, or make love.

as you work, play, or make love. As you unlock this power, you divide your attention. This law comes first for a reason. Divided attention is *the* foundational tool I teach, and mastery of it unlocks new dimensions in a meditative practice.

When you split your attention, you can meditate *while* you do all that stuff that used to stress you out. In fact, until you use a conscious practice to observe yourself, you're on a kind of autopilot. Asleep at the wheel of your life. As you divide your attention though, you rocket into the reality of the present

◇◇◇◇◇◇◇◇◇◇◇◇◇◇◇◇◇◇◇◇◇◇◇◇◇◇◇◇
When you split your attention, you can meditate while you do all that stuff that used to stress you out.
◇◇◇◇◇◇◇◇◇◇◇◇◇◇◇◇◇◇◇◇◇◇◇◇◇◇◇◇

moment. When you're here, you create space, pause, and choice. In this state, you can quite literally dissolve thoughts that trouble you, and focus fully on the moment. So, while you're doing, observe.

I know divided attention sounds complex, so let me show you what it looks like. Recently, I was on a negotiation call with a client. Enticed by her project, I'd come up with a bottom-line price, but my client-to-be offered a lower number. I used to take offense and race to anger at lowballs, thinking, "Don't you know my value?" In this moment, though, I split my attention to view myself on the phone and wonder, "Do I want to take this contract, even at a lower price?" It turns out I did! When you divide your focus this way, you have a powerful tool to make conscious, split-second decisions.

So, an ability to divide your attention is a key tool to live a meditative life. As Michael Singer wrote in *The Untethered Soul*, "you are not the voice of the mind—you are the one who hears it." In the same way, you are not the doer of all the actions—you are the one who observes them. The real you is the soul, possessed of the ability to float above body and brain to observe. This refined part of you views with no attachment or preferences, in total surrender to what is. How

◇◇◇◇◇◇◇◇◇◇◇◇◇◇◇◇◇◇◇◇◇◇◇◇◇◇◇◇◇◇◇◇

The real you is the soul, possessed of the ability to float above body and brain to observe.

◇◇◇◇◇◇◇◇◇◇◇◇◇◇◇◇◇◇◇◇◇◇◇◇◇◇◇◇◇◇◇◇

harmonious your life is correlates to the level of access you have to this part of yourself. With a consistent effort to divide your attention you can weave blissed-out stillness into moments of stress, joy, or sorrow.

Last year, I worked with a client who lived in L.A. Like lots of Angelenos stuck in freeway traffic, she tended to stress out behind the steering wheel. She also drove *a lot,* so it posed a serious problem. As we worked through this law together, though, she started to split her attention as she drove. Over time, she was able to cultivate a meditative state in the midst of L.A. traffic! What's the takeaway? Well, it's so easy to meditate on a mountaintop. Chirping birds. Clean air. Pretty forests. How hard is that? The ability to cultivate calm in car-honking chaos, on the other hand, is a true spiritual tool for everyday use.

In fact, one day as she split her attention on the 405, she imagined herself in her dream ride, a Range Rover, the one she knew she couldn't afford. In our next session, I told her to shift focus to *how* she could afford the car, not convince herself she couldn't buy it. Several weeks later, she found herself behind the wheel of a brand-new, shiny Range Rover. Using meditation, asking, and my help, she clarified expenses versus income, and realized she had been able to afford her dream ride all long. She'd simply been denying herself the pleasure.

Live Above the Law of Divided Attention

To begin dividing your attention, see yourself float to the top of a room, or even the sky. As you do, hold a first-person point of view, too. In other words, float above to see yourself live an experience *and* live that experience right now. Both attentions are essential. In this state, to illustrate, you don't just gaze into a human's eyes. You gaze into her eyes *and* gaze into your own open eyes from above. It's a little meta, I know. It takes some getting used to. You'll know you hit peak split attention, though, when you sense a crisp, clear, calm and stray thoughts disappear.

After the countless hours I spent nodding off or dope sick as a junkie, it took a long time to cultivate the art of split attention. Almost two years, in fact. At first, I started small. I asked myself, "Where are you right now, Biet?" For a long time, I answered, "Not here." I wasn't present to the moment, but that was okay! The ability to see I was asleep, just reacting to the world around me, was so valuable. Over time, as I recognized this sleep state, I started to wake myself up by dividing my attention.

As you cultivate this practice, check in like clockwork. Set an alarm on your phone and label it, "divide your attention." When it goes off, ask yourself, "Where am I right now?" It doesn't matter the answer. It took me years to get to a point where I could regularly answer, "I'm here." So, split your attention to cultivate peak focus and calm, but be patient with yourself. No beat-ups! Awakening is about awareness, not judgment. Anytime you notice you're not present, it's a new opportunity to grow.

Verification Point

Observe from above in this very moment, and see yourself through the eyes of a loved one, tender and compassionate. As you go about your day, split your attention as often as possible. In the car, watch yourself drive, even as you view the road ahead. In a heated conversation, observe yourself as you argue. See a pouty frown or nasty look. Once you really *see* yourself angry, you'll probably calm down pretty quickly.

2

THE LAW OF AIM

If you've ever been in love, you'll recognize the feeling. Colors seem brighter. Life seems effortless, worries disappear, and joy fills your heart like it's on a bottomless tap. Though the euphoria of being in love is fleeting, meditation can make the sensation almost automatic, as it releases joy into our lives *right now*. When you journey into your inner world to meditate and awaken conscious, you connect to your soul and usher in bliss, gratitude, and intention—what I call the state of love. *To cultivate and maintain this state is your primary aim on planet earth.* And you don't even need to be *in* love to experience it. Sounds great, right?

Well, let me tell you about secondary aims. These are our worldly goals, ambitions, and dreams. Nothing wrong with them at all. In fact, there's a lot to like! A second home in Montauk, the perfect life partner, a seven-figure bank account, six-pack abs, beautiful and healthy children, your dream job, vacations in Turks and Caicos. The problem is, sometimes we put our secondary aims first, and treat them as our primary aim. We worry, stress, or manipulate situations to try and reach our goals, which leaves us feeling burned out and unsatisfied even when we grab the brass ring.

When we're driven only by secondary aims, we often can't enjoy longed-for goals because of the emotional states we've churned up. Or, our joy is fleeting and after a few hours or days, we're out striving for the next goal. Think about it. Have you ever known or heard of someone who "has it all" but can't quite seem to ever enjoy it? The list is long. This makes sense, because putting secondary aims into the driver's seat of our lives is emotionally and physically exhausting.

Okay, so how do you balance your long-term goals and daily priorities with a conscious state of calm, bliss, and gratitude? The answer is not easy, but it is simple: honor the state of love as your primary aim. Sit in meditation to begin every day. If you're new to the practice, sit for at least fifteen minutes, perhaps using the techniques I laid out in "Meditation 101." Then throughout your day, whether on an early morning conference call, hiking in the mountains, or dropping your kids off at school, practice asking and breathe in through your nose to stay in a conscious state.

Here's the best part: an awakened life brings our material goals and ambitions into sharper focus, shows us how to enjoy them, and makes us available to receive opportunities *beyond* our wildest dreams. This is the way we start to turn *the* primary aim into *our* primary aim. How? Let me tell you a story.

In my twenties, I was obsessed with fame. I also happened to be a junkie, so I spent a lot of my free time snorting speedballs off of toilets with literal rock stars, celebrities, and models in graffitied nightclub bathrooms on the Lower East Side of Manhattan. My secondary aim? Fame. My primary aim? Nowhere in sight. At the time, I held a very clear vision: performing the music I wrote at world-class museums across the globe, starting with my hometown favorite, the Museum of Modern Art (MoMA). Signed to Sony Records at the time, I thought that with my talent and record deal, all I needed to do was mix with the right crowd, make the right connections, and presto: I'd be the next Björk.

It didn't quite turn out that way. One night, I found myself sitting in a New York City jail cell, high as a kite, with almost a thousand dollars of heroin and cocaine stashed in my purse. How I got there is a story for another time. Suffice it to say, it wasn't pretty. Anyway, as I sat on the jail cell toilet, I asked my father's spirit to keep the cops' eyes off my bag. I know, I know. Foxhole prayers. That's how I used to use the tool of asking. Misguided, I was. In the end, they released me without ever searching my bag, but that's where blind focus on secondary aim led me. Granted, my story is a little extreme, but it makes the point pretty clearly.

When I got sober and meditated inward to touch my soul, I began to live in a state of love again. Guided by intention, I developed the system I teach now and unearthed my true desire to perform and lead meditations at museums across the world. As I spread my work to larger audiences, I held this vision as a secondary aim, and guided by a rigorous daily meditation practice, built an intentional life. Fast forward a few years to last spring, and where do you think I led a meditation and sang a cappella for a crowd of six hundred? That's right: MoMA! Today, I regularly lead large-scale meditations there, and at retreats and summits at boutique hotels, resorts, and dreamy destination spots across the globe.

As you read this, you may be saying, "I don't have time to culti-vate the state of *love*, for fuck's sake. Have you *seen* my calendar?" This kind of thinking is typical to a "time is not my friend," sec-ondary aim mind-set. There are other indicators you are driven primarily by worldly aims. You may avert the present moment as if it were the plague, worrying about the future or thinking about the past. Feeling misunderstood or alone, you worry that you won't discover or live out your life's purpose. You may have a very hard time admitting what you want. Or you may be very clear about what you want, but keep it a secret and believe you're not quite worthy of having it.

Live Above the Law of Aim

The shift into primary aim means that you choose a conscious meditative state—asking, breathing, divided attention—as your first priority, even on the busiest days. This choice allows the state of love to govern your dreams and ambitions, instead of allowing your goals to govern your thoughts and emotions. In this state, you will clarify the secondary aims you really care about and ac-tually enjoy the path to achieving them. I once heard a comedian say, "I used to think success was popping bottles of cham-pagne while I counted my millions. Today, I know it's a succession of millions of beautiful moments, one after another." Above this law, you have a singular focal point at all times made of invisible light. When your aim

> The shift into primary aim means that you choose a conscious meditative state—asking, breathing, divided attention—as your first priority, even on the busiest days.

This choice allows the state of love to govern your dreams and ambitions, instead of allowing your goals to govern your thoughts and emotions.

is to be connected to this point at all times, you will see how nothing in your circumstances matters. You are safe and free.

Verification Point

Note when an event seems to drag you from your primary aim and you're frustrated or irritable. A delayed flight. A pushy client. See how easy it is to divert from your primary aim. Pause, breathe deeply, and use the tool of asking: "How would I choose to *be* in this moment if my primary aim were to stay in a state of love?"

If you can't pull that off at first, no worries! Just noticing when you're frazzled is verification enough. As you continue to see how easily secondary aims drag you away from the primary, you'll tire of it. Choose to ask, meditate, and split attentions in moments of stress. As you flex spiritual muscles, they get stronger, and soon you'll be able to summon serenity and calmness at will. In your journal, write an affirmation ten times: "No matter the circumstance, my primary aim is to connect to the Divine."

3

THE LAW OF IDENTIFICATION

My assistant showed up this morning at my home bearing gifts: a toothy smile, cold brew coffee from my fave local place, and copies of this month's *Elle* and *Harper's Bazaar*. Today marks the publication of my first feature interview in *Harper's*, and the article refers to me as an om girl, like "it girl" but for meditation. I've been labeled before: *Forbes* called me a meditation guru, and in this month's write-up, *Elle* referred to me as a high-end meditation guide. It would be easy to identify with these monikers, to assume them as my true identity. I get so much joy from my work as a spiritual teacher, but I do not believe that is what I *am*.

Okay. Why am I telling you this?

We often identify ourselves with our careers, how others see us, our personalities, or the results we get. Nothing wrong with that, right? Well, a little. Labels like wife, entrepreneur, Chris Rock of meditation (it's true, a man at one of my events actually called me that) are examples of the Law of Identification in action, and, while they are quite normal, they can be dangerous in unskilled hands. Of course, there is nothing wrong with being called a high-end guru, especially for a girl who grew up in Jackson Heights! *But the more we wrap our identity in labels, the less likely we are to identify with who we truly are: our soul, our consciousness.*

A famous prayer attributed to St. Francis of Assisi tells us, "it is in self-forgetting that one finds." In order to discover our true identity in the soul, we have to stop clinging to our professional, personal, and familial identities. In this sense, we must "forget" ourselves. This is a tremendously freeing experience. When we shed our attachment to identifying as pretty or homely, rich or poor, fit or fat—any identity at all, really—we are free to create and design our lives from the most powerful source available: the soul.

The real me is the soul, communicating with divine consciousness. Then there's Biet, my soul's proxy here on planet earth. As my ambassador, she's witty, gentle, and kind, and at times insecure, doubtful, and sad. When I lived inside of Biet as if I was her, I suffered greatly. I wanted everyone to like me, I wanted to look a certain way and feel pitch-perfect all the time. I take care of Biet so she's healthy and beautiful. Biet has moods, I do not. I observe her, and let her have all the moods she wants, and through meditation/observing, I bring her back to the true state of love and bliss, the neutral calm of the soul. Today, I don't give a shit if everyone likes me.

> The real me is the soul, communicating with divine consciousness. Then there's Biet, my soul's proxy here on planet earth.

When we identify with something, we find it difficult to let it go. This makes life unnecessarily painful. If we identify with being young and beautiful, we are going to find the aging process intolerable. If we identify as part of a relationship and that relationship dissolves, we will struggle to move on because we no longer feel whole. If we identify with a job and lose it, we may feel lost and aimless. But when we remember who we are and identify only with our souls, we

> But when we remember who we are and identify only with our souls, we can move through life with ease.

can move through life with ease. We no longer feel pain because we can never lose the soul. The soul is who we are.

This law works on more immediate, short-term levels, as well. Sometimes, we find ourselves so wrapped up in a project, task, or object that we forget our true selves. If you're on your way to the Hamptons from the Upper West Side, and traffic snarls make it a five-hour trip, you can respond in one of two ways. If you've identified with arriving by a specific time, you'll panic or get angry. "What the fuck is going on? I have somewhere to be!" If you're not identified with the result, you can take the event in stride and find a more productive, perhaps even enjoyable, way to navigate the situation.

This law can also limit us to identify as victims of circumstance. The uneducated person might be incapable of seeing herself as someone with a college degree, so she settles for a low-paying job because she can't imagine a life in which she achieves her lifelong dream of becoming an architect. The obese man might sabotage his own efforts to lose weight because he identifies with a larger body. When he thinks of himself, he cannot picture himself thin. If I had not had the spiritual foundation my father gave me, I very well may have continued to identify as a grief-stricken, orphan junkie. I could never have envisioned a world in which I was sober and thriving.

You can also see you're identified with something if you feel pain whenever it is threatened. If you've ever turned into a self-loathing basket case after receiving a slight criticism from your boss, that's a sure sign that you identify with your career, or being perfect. If you identify as being intelligent, you'll chastise yourself for being stupid if you're ever proven wrong. If you've given up on a dream because you think it's not possible, you're likely too identified with your life as it is. If you identify as a happy person, you might berate yourself when you feel sad or angry.

One of my clients, the CEO at a thriving tech start-up, was a player. A handsome and successful man in his early forties, he was infatuated with his ability to romance, date, and sleep with younger women. Identified as a pickup artist, he actually craved a wife and kids. The real problem, though, was he couldn't see his own intrinsic desirability. He used one-night stands to experience himself as desirable. As we meditated together, I guided the guy to observe himself from the soul's point of view, where he experienced the sheer pleasure of his inherent value as a man. As he saw this intrinsic value, late night flirts and flings began to fall away. He met the girl of his dreams, to whom he's now married. Their first child is due next year.

Live Above the Law of Identification

Identified with career, relationships, or your results, you mask the soul. That makes it hard for all the other souls riding around this planet in bodies to experience your true power. So, start to distinguish between those words and actions that are identified, and those that reflect who you really are. Identified thoughts and feelings tend to create nervousness and tension; unidentified thoughts present as calm and neutral. When you begin to practice the latter, you'll begin to live above this law, and the things you used to identify with will be a kind of playtime, a source of joy rather than stress. A strong dose of meditation helps on this front, naturally.

Verification Point

Notice moments when one of your identities is threatened. See how attached you are to things going "your way." Consider that this may be identification at work, and take a moment to observe ways you identify. You may identify as a "winner," so if you lose, your very identity is threatened. If you identify as "right," when you're wrong you may become angry. Ask to recognize these moments in meditation on and off your cushion, and split your attentions when they arise to come back to the present. In your journal, write a list of three to five ways you're currently identified. For each one, describe the freedom available to you when you make the choice to let go of these identifications.

4

THE LAW OF SHOCKS

I used to fall in love to shock myself awake, always seeking a higher state. In my junkie rock 'n' roll days, I even wrote a song called "Famous for Falling in Love"! Shocks like falling in love or the birth of a child wake you up to a rare moment where you're fully alert and alive, with a keen sense of urgency about your mission on planet earth. A near-death experience or the untimely death of a loved one can propel you into this awakened state, too. Nerves wake you up. So do tears. But what if I told you that you can call on this peak awake sense at will? It's true! You can actually trigger a state of conscious presence, and sync to the most exuberant, productive version of you.

◇◇◇◇◇◇◇◇◇◇◇◇◇◇◇◇◇◇◇◇◇◇◇◇

You can actually trigger a state of conscious presence, and sync to the most exuberant, productive version of you.

◇◇◇◇◇◇◇◇◇◇◇◇◇◇◇◇◇◇◇◇◇◇◇◇

So many times, people confuse meditation with calm and relaxation. In fact, meditation is meant to shock you out of ordinary rhythms into a new state of consciousness. Since the mind and body lull us into a kind of robotic routine akin to being asleep, it's vital to shock ourselves into new states if we're to awaken. Enlightenment is really one giant shock to a status quo state of mind.

So, how do you create conscious shocks? One way is to take actions that push you outside your comfort zone. Take a long walk with a close friend in total silence. Sit in front of a beautiful painting at a museum, gaze at it for at least twenty minutes, and breathe in through your nose, deep into the diaphragm, then out through your mouth. Jump out of an airplane (use a parachute). Sit cross-legged, knee to knee with a friend or lover, and gaze into his or her eyes. Attend a silent retreat. Fast. Take a spontaneous trip. Notice the heightened state of perception you create.

Smaller actions can also trigger conscious shocks. Choose a different route to and from work every day for a week. Walk barefoot on grass or a sandy beach. Brush your teeth with your nondominant hand. Scribe a page-long journal entry with that same hand. Notice how slow and intentional you need to be, and how the practice ushers you into the present. Choose a cuisine you've never tasted before, and sample a new delicacy. Watch a conscious film, one that tells the story of the soul's awakening, such as *The Truman Show, The Matrix*, or *Wings of Desire.*

You can also use moments of transition to usher in states of presence. When you open a door to a new space, say a small prayer, and ask to be ushered into a state of presence. Use phone calls as a similar opportunity. Before you answer a call or push the call button yourself, ask to be gifted generosity, compassion, and loving-kindness. If you're deep in thought at a project or task at work or home, and someone calls out to you, use the same ask to prep for a state change, shift into a new, conscious gear, and leave the task behind for a moment.

The power of heartbreak is also potent, as the shock of a breakup ushers us into an altered state where we have access to heightened creative powers. In fact, some of the greatest albums of all time were birthed in a breakup. There's a whole genre to it: the breakup album! Subconsciously, I think it's why some people fall in love, then break up over and over again. In the absence of a spiritual practice, it's like they've discovered a mechanism they can use to shock themselves into a state of presence. To be clear, don't go break up with lovers to shock yourself into a state of presence! It's not a sustainable method to create shocks. Plus, you have meditation. Go meditate!

Live Above the Law of Shocks

To live above this law, notice what tools you're using to create shocks. Are you doing what I used to do, breaking hearts or losing love? These aftershocks are the by-product of a relationship with another soul, and instead we want to cultivate the ability to create our own shocks. Using the methods I presented above, start to build a toolkit for consciously shocking yourself every day into a state of presence. Of course, a steady diet of meditation and asking is a key part of our ability to achieve this state, so make sure your daily practices are in order first.

The more you create intentional shocks for yourself, the less the universe will give you accidental ones. Also, if you're like most people, your shocks won't be as intense as mine. In order to wake up, I had to become a drug addict, my dad and baby had to die, and my house had to

◇◇◇◇◇◇◇◇◇◇◇◇◇◇◇◇◇◇◇◇◇◇◇◇
The more you create intentional shocks for yourself, the less the universe will give you accidental ones.
◇◇◇◇◇◇◇◇◇◇◇◇◇◇◇◇◇◇◇◇◇◇◇◇

burn down. Some of us just need to get frustrated at work, or go through a bad breakup. That can be enough of a shock.

Verification Point

During moments of transition, split your attentions to shock yourself awake to the present moment. Ask, or pray, before you make a call, and when you receive one. Before you enter a conference room at an office, or when you come home from a long day, pause, breathe, and bring yourself into the present. When you use transitions as a spiritual tool, you can create pockets of calm stillness in the middle of a busy day.

When you use transitions as a spiritual tool, you can create pockets of calm stillness in the middle of a busy day.

5

THE LAW OF THREE

Mind, body, soul. Brahma, Shiva, Vishnu. Father, Son, Holy Spirit. Spiritual harmony comes in threes, yet so often we're stuck in a one, two step dance of desire, then denying force—any difficulty, big or small, that pushes you to give up or change course. One, you go for a goal. Two, denying force arises. For every action, there is an equal and opposite reaction. Even *if* you get what you want, though, the prize is now you have new desires and new difficulties. It's like a hamster wheel. So, the trick is to intro a third force: the soul's blissed-out neutrality. It's real; I meditate to get neutral. In this altered state, you can float above wants, obstacles, and successes alike.

First, though, we need to talk about denying force. In pursuit of any aim, you're going to face it. A star basketball player signs a $100 million contract, then breaks an ankle five minutes into his first game. A writer fulfills a lifelong dream: she's staffed on a hot new Netflix series! Six months later, it's canceled. A man falls in love with his dream girl. She cheats on him. What's really wild is, think of all the difficulties and near deal breakers they persisted past to get to their goal in the first place. The point is, denying force doesn't quit.

Let's say you want a huge house in the Hollywood Hills because, really, who doesn't? You come up with profitable ideas, sacrifice a social life, skip a family, save your money. Though you know on some level it's not true, you may say, "Once I get that house, it's smooth sailing from here on out. Yippee!" Finally, the big day arrives. You move in and marvel at the view. You've arrived. Fast forward a few months, though, and the picture is quite different. You're used to the house you dreamed about. Now, new denying force

> The hometown hip-hop hero hit on a key axiom of this law: *nothing outside your soul will ever free you from denying force.*

presents. It didn't go anywhere. It just mutated. Property taxes. Remodels. Earthquakes. Stress. Worries. Anxiety. Biggie Smalls said it best: "Mo money, mo problems." The hometown hip-hop hero hit on a key axiom of this law: *nothing outside your soul will ever free you from denying force.*

So, what can you do? Well, you can kick-start a kind of "above it all" neutrality that dissolves the one, two step dance of desire and denying force. Stop being selective with life, cherry-picking experiences you want, and saying, "No, thanks" to the ones you don't. Open yourself to what life brings *no matter what.* Free yourself from the tiresome struggle that demands life be the way you want it. In this state, you can float above sadness or joy, tragedy or success, love or heartbreak. Denying force can't really deny you when you're open to all life brings. If you've ever wanted to live on the edge, this is the way to do it.

In this way, you form an unbreakable triad, one you can use

as long as you live. You can enjoy desires and know denying force, but tap the soul's power to neutralize ups and downs. It's like Einstein said, "No problem can be solved from the same level of consciousness that created it." To level up, you can use this neutral "third eye" to observe yourself as you succeed, fail, suffer, or triumph. The triad that the neutral soul forms with desire and denying force reveals reality to us, and it's how we find freedom.

Years ago, I catered ultra-fancy galas in and around Manhattan for $20 an hour. Uptown townhouses. Hamptons estates. Mansions upstate. I spent my shifts waiting for midnight, when I stole a bottle of whiskey, and our crew of tuxedoed caterers walked off into the woods to get shitfaced. Then, I woke up hungover and tried to practice the law of attraction. Spoiler alert: it didn't work. Trapped by the dance between denying force and desire, I'd wonder, "How am I supposed to feel rich when I have no money?" I just didn't get it. Not only did it not work, I actually started to hate the idea that I could "manifest" a life I loved. It made me visibly upset, because I was totally unable to do it at the time

Desperate for money when I was sober years later, I catered again. As the seeds of the work I do now took root, I asked God how I could neutralize the money I wanted, the poverty I hated. A few days later, a novel idea popped into my brain. I could use catering as an opportunity to practice client service skills! It sounded weird, but I did it anyway. Whenever I offered a guest a mealy crab cake, which they usually declined, I pretended I was making a sale to a client. I started to use catering as a kind of playground, one where I could get comfy with "selling" and rejection. Then I took it a step further.

As I served tiny hors d'oeuvres on big platters, I imagined myself an invited guest, a famous meditation guru with a book published at Simon & Schuster. "These are my friends," I thought.

"This is my house, those are my cars, and this is my life." I started to enjoy catering so much my friends thought I was crazy. One sunny summer day at a party in the Hamptons, a nattily dressed woman sidled up to me and asked me what I thought of the crowd. She had mistaken me for a guest! It was pretty comical, really, as I was kitted out in a cheap polyester rent-a-tux, but it showed me I could shift reality.

So, what's the point? I badly wanted to have enough money to live well, but I was stuck in a cycle of poverty I couldn't escape. When I asked to be neutral to the wealth I wanted and the poverty I had, I floated above denying force and desire. Fueled by this third force, I saw catering with new eyes, leading to a breakthrough. I'd been afraid to be so confident, scared others would think me arrogant. Now, I wasn't confident in *me*, in my work along the horizontal line. I was confident in the vertical line power I tapped, the same energy that's available to everybody. So, it wasn't even really about me. No me, no arrogance. Today, I return to many of the same sites I catered, but now as a guest!

Live Above the Law of Three

To live above the Law of Three, expect denying force as a matter of course. When you know it will come, you'll no longer be surprised when it hits. So often, we live in fantasy, and expect ourselves to realize desires without a hitch. Then we complain or feel sorry for ourselves when obstacles arise. When you see that the level of denying force stays constant in your life at all times, it's going to bother you a lot less.

As you come to expect denying force, start to see where you can form triads. Perhaps you're a big-time doer and you achieve a lot, pushing past denying force with brute strength. If so, look to

If so, look to see where you can catch a kind of spiritual wind in your meditation, so you can spend more time gliding like an elegant eagle, and less time flapping your wings. If you're more passive and tend to surrender to denying force, ask for clarity to see how much you matter in the world. Forge forward even when denying force hits.

Verification Point

In order to verify this law in your life, practice being neutral in your responses to reality. When you receive bad news, greet it with the same enthusiasm and gratitude you'd show to great news. Be curious and wonder, "What opportunity is available here that I can't see yet?" Then, look for answers as you meditate. Really, an awakened state is the ability to react newly to the same events that used to trouble us.

6

THE LAW OF SELF-REMEMBERING

At the climax of *The Matrix*—a parable about the awakening of the soul set in a computer simulation—the hero, an "average Joe" programmer turned conscious being, stands in a hallway. Just nearly killed, in a flash, his hundreds of hours of training explode in a moment of clarity. Suddenly awake inside the simulation, he sees all around him—hallways, doors, enemy agents—not as it appears, but as it *is*: green lines of code across a black screen. In this state, he sees his true purpose as "The One," savior of humanity. He has bent the rules of reality and lives above the laws of the universe. When the agents fire bullets at him, he stops the bullets, plucks one out of the air, and then drops the rest to the floor. He flies. He has self-remembered.

Self-remembering is the highest experiential state a human can attain on planet earth. Often immensely pleasurable, in this state of deep awakening we tend to be acutely present to all five senses at once, and filled with a deep sense of serenity. We usually experience a cosmic awareness, that a divine presence links all humans together in an unbroken chain of shared consciousness.

A conscious shock to your system, self-remembering is akin to a kind of celestial experience. Pleasure and pain, joy and sadness, love and anger all meld into one sensation, shattering the illusion of separateness.

⟨⟨⟨⟨⟨⟨⟨⟨⟨⟨⟨⟨⟨⟨⟨⟨⟨⟨⟨⟨⟨⟨⟨⟨⟨

A conscious shock to your system, self-remembering is akin to a kind of celestial experience.

⟨⟨⟨⟨⟨⟨⟨⟨⟨⟨⟨⟨⟨⟨⟨⟨⟨⟨⟨⟨⟨⟨⟨⟨⟨

Living under this law, though, you feel mediocre, numb, or bored. You may leave the present moment often, and spend most of your energy mulling over the past or worrying about the future. You may yearn for things you feel you cannot have, but don't put forth any effort to get them. In a state of forgetfulness, you spend energy on things that are not important while putting off things that you desire most. You may believe your life has no meaning. As soon as you feel like your life is without purpose, you have forgotten yourself.

I used to only be able to glimpse moments of self-remembering when I ate hallucinogenic mushrooms or kissed someone I was in love with for the first time. In fact, you may remember yourself during a shock—a near-death experience, sexual climax, falling in love—where you *know* that all things are possible. However divine these moments may be, they are fleeting. As soon as the euphoria passes, you forget yourself, and return to a kind of autopilot state. You can cultivate your ability to remember yourself, though, by using the tool of divided attention. Split attentions allow you to remember yourself in a sustained and steady way, instead of only glimpsing the state in orgasm or, say, on a plant medicine like ayahuasca.

In his book *Catching the Big Fish*, filmmaker David Lynch writes that when we dive deep into our consciousness, we leave the realm of the guppies and pull out the whale. For Lynch, the guppies represent pedestrian mediocrity, while the whale expresses the highest self, clear purpose, and unleashed creative powers—a state of self-remembering. Certain conscious beings throughout history pulled out the whale: philosophers and spiritual teachers such as Jesus, Plato, the Buddha, but also painters, composers, and politicians like Rembrandt, Bach, and Abraham Lincoln, humans who plugged into the spiritual mainframe of the universe to bring back world-changing contributions in art, music, and politics. To be clear, though, you don't have to become the Buddha or Bach to pull out the whale. Sometimes, self-remembering seizes us in the most ordinary moments. The trick is to make yourself available to receive it.

One sunny morning, after attending one of my meditation workshops at the Museum of Modern Art, a young woman walked out into the rush-hour streets of midtown Manhattan. In a state of bliss after a series of divided attention gazing exercises during the session, she decided to approach strangers hurrying to and fro, look them in the eyes, and say "hello." Most people ignored her. Eventually, she approached a well-dressed elderly man in a suit and tie, briefcase in hand, on the corner of 57th and Madison. She looked him in the eye, said "hello," and he looked directly at her and responded, "I've been waiting for you."

A jaded New Yorker, she stepped back, but he explained he had been standing on the corner for an hour. A man of considerable wealth, he wanted to give a great gift that day, paying off the debt of the first person he saw who showed him a sign that they were the one. Still skeptical, but burdened with over $60,000 in student loans, she exchanged email addresses with the man, and he asked her to send him her loan account numbers. Later, thinking it might be some kind of scam, she decided not to follow through, and the next day, he emailed her, asking, "Why are you keeping yourself from receiving this gift?" "All right, fine. Fuck it," she thought, and sensing the man's sincerity and well-heeled demeanor, she pulled up her student loan accounts, threw in a few credit card payoffs for good measure, and forwarded the account numbers to him. Hours later, she received an email from her loan provider thanking her for her payment, and stating her loan was paid in full. She checked her credit cards: zero balance.

Miraculous story, right? To be clear, I'm not suggesting that you go around saying hello to strangers in the street and hope they give you money. Through divided attention meditation, the young woman from our story accessed a state of self-remembering. When she set out to look strangers in the eye, student loans were perhaps the furthest thing from her mind. Rather, in a state of inspired presence, she simply sought to deliver to other humans the value of truly being seen. During midtown Manhattan rush hour no less! The point is to practice cultivating a state of self-remembering via meditation and divided attention. Who knows what miracles await?

◇◇◇◇◇◇◇◇◇◇◇◇◇◇◇◇◇◇◇◇◇◇◇◇◇◇◇◇◇
Who knows what miracles await?
◇◇◇◇◇◇◇◇◇◇◇◇◇◇◇◇◇◇◇◇◇◇◇◇◇◇◇◇◇

Live Above the Law of Self-Remembering

Use the tool of divided attention to try to acquire self-remembering. With meditation and conscious breathing, practice staying in the present moment. When a rush of self-remembering first hits, it will feel profound and dramatic, like a fire burning through your body giving you the energy to accomplish anything. But even when you put in the effort, self-remembering is not guaranteed. It is a divine gift, and you can't force it. In the beginning of your work with this law, you will pass in and out of remembering and forgetting, mostly living in forgetting; but the more you practice, the closer you will come to a consistent state of self-remembering.

Verification Point

In your journal, keep track of miracles, or moments of self-remembering. I think of miracles as serendipitous experiences, ones where you put forth little or no effort. Think of our friend with student loans. The miracles don't need to be on that scale, but it's essential to record serendipitous moments in a small notebook you carry everywhere. And don't use your phone; these are meant to be stored in a sacred place. One day, if you have a really bad day, this list will be surprisingly useful!

7

THE LAW OF PERSONALITY

Have you hugged Amma? Known as the hugging saint, this adorable Indian guru draws crazy huge crowds that queue for hours for the opportunity simply to hug her. Why? Well, when I hug her, I'm filled with a light energy, presence, and calm that transcends the ordinary moment. Somewhat heavyset, sporting flowing white robes, a nose ring, and a kind smile, Amma's authenticity is so powerful I've seen a grown man weep in her arms.

Souls like hers express the quality of authentic personality. She's freed herself from the tyranny of false personality, a key force that limits our full self-expression and sense of purpose here on planet earth. You don't have to become a hugging guru to shed false personality, but you must work to uncover your true one; *no one can tell the story of your soul better than your personality.*

> *No one can tell the story of your soul better than your personality.*

Personality encompasses all of your choices: ways you act,

likes and dislikes, what you wear, character traits, where you live, people you surround yourself with. It is also a mixture of your memories, personal history, and what you do for fun. Acquired via experience, personality is a layer next to the soul that helps you interact with life. In the same way that no two thumbprints are alike, no two personalities are, either. No one else can ever become *you*, because your personality is so specifically nuanced and unique. Sometimes, though, we acquire personality traits or entire personalities that are not a reflection of our true selves—false personality.

False personality tends to express itself as traits and ways of being that don't jibe with our authentic selves. Typically, these are traits we've acquired at some point from family members, colleagues, or friends. You may really want to date someone, but when they text, you take hours to reply because you think this makes you seem cool, or more desirable. You may be kind and generous, but in a high-stakes boardroom presentation, you try to impress your audience with showy, cocky moves. Some of these choices may pay off in the short term, but in the long term they tend to be ineffective and leave us drained and dissatisfied. Worrying about what others think, you may not recognize your own greatness. In other words, under false personality, you're trying to be someone who really isn't you.

When I was young, I imitated my father. Strutting around in his underwear all day on weekends, he drank vodka, made love to many women, and blew money on caviar. Modeling his behavior, I was a bit of a dilettante. I didn't value money, and had very little of it. What I did have was hours upon hours of free time, and I slowly walked around the city, taking in art and reading philosophical texts slow and on repeat. I met friends for leisurely tea dates, or out at weeknight parties till the wee hours of the morning. I snorted piles of heroin. I ended up super-depressed.

You see, I thought I was supposed to be this utopian dreamer with no valuation for material possessions or achievement, but this was false personality.

Well, it turns out I'm actually an overachiever. Via meditation and the exploration of these laws, I discovered I had been hiding this ambitious nature in the closet. If you'd asked me if I was ambitious, I would have told you "not really," which was a lie, but I wouldn't have even *known* that then. I would've thought I was telling you the truth.

Today, I wear my personality like an outfit.

There's nothing *wrong* with the person I pretended to be back then—other than the heroin! The dreamer who values free time and spends hours in conversation is a perfect person to be. But it wasn't the whole *me*.

Today, *I wear my personality like an outfit*. When I discovered the story of my soul was to become the woman I am today, I realized my personality was the perfect vehicle. I love to shop at Barneys. I drink $10 cold-pressed juices. I binge watch *Twin Peaks*. I rock tight bangs. I grew up in Manhattan rock clubs. I have an edgy sense of humor. These aspects of my personality allow me to reach audiences who might never have meditated before. They're a vital feature of the vessel that presents my soul's message. My personality is super well-suited to bring meditative consciousness to fashion, music, and other aspects of the modern world. My personality tells the story of my soul.

My personality tells the story of my soul.

Live Above the Law of Personality

Begin to "live in the question." Be curious, and use the tool of divided attention to watch yourself, asking questions like, "Is this really me?" Experiment with different ways of being. Be kind in a situation others may think calls for ego and dominance. Be authentic, responding quickly to your crush's text message. Stay away from argument, regardless of how right you feel you are. If you do argue and "lose," worry not. The party that "loses" an argument actually wins, as they're the one who walks away with a new, possibly valuable idea. Notice expressions of your personality that generate a quiet calm, as this inner state tends to signal aspects of true personality. Once you've identified these states, from a position of power you can consistently choose to live in them.

Verification Point

This is a good time to get creative. Perhaps the way you appear right now is not your fullest self-expression. Maybe you're not meant to look like the pop star Pink, exactly, but I bet you're not fully waving your own freak flag either. So, go get the haircut you always wanted or a fabulous new outfit. Something that expresses the real *you*. Get gussied up and wear your new threads the next time you go to buy groceries. Start to suit up every day as if each moment is the most important one in your life. Because it is! Once you do this, you will verify that it feels better to be the real you.

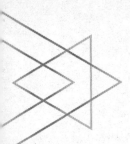

8

THE LAW OF EQUALS

Raise your hand if you've ever been jealous. My hand's up. Anyone else? No need to beat yourself up. It's a natural human emotion! Usually when you get jealous, guilt and frustration come along for the ride, and if you don't grasp the valuable opportunity jealousy offers, that makes sense. By itself, it's a rather nasty emotion. But what if I told you that jealousy is a tool you can use to locate your equals on this planet? Your community. Your circle. Your crew. When you understand that flares of jealousy point you toward your equals, it's a game changer.

> What if I told you that jealousy is a tool you can use to locate your equals on this planet?

When I was in high school, I was jealous of a few friends. Of course, I didn't know they were my equals at the time; I thought they were prettier, wittier, and smarter. Years later, these friends I was jealous of? They're all killing it at life! Big careers. Big joy. Big luck. In other words, jealousy is designed to guide you to humans who can boost you to dream big and get to your goals. It's a wild idea, I know. Jealousy is so scary to most people, it's on a list called the Seven Deadly Sins! I promise you, though, there's nothing to fear. *Jealousy is a compass, not a threat.*

Today, as soon as I even suspect the faintest bit of jealousy, I know that I've met an equal: a true friend, and a partner who will lovingly challenge me to rise to my highest potential. A peer who has my back. These great friends push each other! Inspire each other! Raise the bar together! If you look around your life and think, "That guy's above me. He's way too cool, too successful. Out of my league," that may just be a sign you're his equal. In fact, since jealousy creates equals, and equals form the deepest, most satisfying friendships, jealousy is kind of the north star of friendship, as well.

Jealousy is a compass, not a threat.

When you find your equals, they inspire you to play your one true note. You finally realize that no one in the whole world can play the same note as you, not even if they tried. Your equals have their own notes, too, and they will play them alongside you. In this community of peers you build, you will play together like a glorious symphony. Whoever told you that enlightenment and joy is something you find walking up a mountain all alone was lying to you. Awakening takes a village. So start getting cozy with your equals. Together, you'll build what no one human could on her own.

When you find your equals, they inspire you to play your one true note.

One day a few years back, a successful entrepreneur sat down on a cushion at a workshop I led in Manhattan. When I saw her,

I was a bit nervous, as I'd admired her from afar for a while. I was a bit jealous, too. She loved the sit session and we chatted afterward, but I still couldn't see us as equals. So I decided to challenge myself and arranged for mutual friends to introduce us at a summer rooftop party in Williamsburg.

That evening, we spoke for hours as I shared the story of my daughter's death and how I kicked heroin. She listened intently, spoke of her own deep secrets and desires, and we wept together. "Wow, we're just equals," I realized in that moment. We're now connected in a deeply intimate community of friends, and I count her as a close friend. We collaborate, coach each other, and create new ideas together. Equals.

Live Above the Law of Equals

To live above this law, start to *use jealousy as a compass*, and let it point you toward your equals. Notice patterns. What do these humans have in common? It may be career trajectory, personality, or some other attribute. So, use your observations to reveal your heart's desire. Alchemize jealousy into a light that illuminates goals and dreams you really want. Realize that when a jealous pang hits, you see your own potential mirrored in an equal's gumption, vigor, and clarity.

In your relationships, start to experience others' joys and successes as if they were your own. When a friend signs a book deal, marries, or sells a successful start-up, sense in meditation what it feels like to experience that moment of triumph. Luxuriate in their bliss. Since we're really all connected anyway, it's yours, too! Strive to spend

◇◇◇◇◇◇◇◇◇◇◇◇◇◇◇◇◇◇◇◇◇◇

Start to experience others' joys and successes as if they were your own.

◇◇◇◇◇◇◇◇◇◇◇◇◇◇◇◇◇◇◇◇◇◇

more time with people you admire, and less time with those who don't challenge you.

Verification Point

Choose someone who gins up jealousy in you, an equal. Ask yourself, "Do I believe I have the potential to create at their level? What would I do if I did believe that?" Then, invite them to a lunch or coffee. Be persistent. If they decline, choose someone else. Have coffee more than once, with a few different people. Look for all the ways you're similar. Over time, these ways will get easier to spot.

9

THE LAW OF SEVEN
(LAW OF SUCCESS)

Seven notes in a musical scale. Seven days in a week. Seven colors in a rainbow. Seven Wonders of the World. The day God rests after creating the universe. Far and away the most popular number, according to research studies. *The Magnificent Seven. The Seven Samurai. The Seventh Seal.* James Bond. Okay, I'm kidding about the last one. But really, why is this digit everywhere we look? Well, according to many spiritual traditions, the number seven is deeply significant. In the work I study, we must pass through key stages to reach success in any endeavor. To explain the process clearly, I'll use an octave in the C major musical scale, *Sound of Music* style: do-re-mi fa-so-la si-do.

In do-re-mi, the first stage of any quest for success, you revel in and anticipate all the "cash and prizes" headed your way. Let's say, for example, you're about to go paleo. In do-re-mi, you can't wait to get super-healthy. You buy all the avocados, pastured bacon fat, and coconut oil your kitchen can hold. Nothing can

52

stop you now. Or, you're kicking around screenplay ideas with a friend, and you land on the perfect one. You see it on the silver screen. You compose the Oscar acceptance speech in your head. It's perfect!

Okay, this is going to sound harsh, so brace yourself. Most humans spend their entire lives in do-re-mi, titillated and all talked out about a dream that they never manifest, in a state of excitement about something they'll never do. Internally, they're saddled with sadness around never moving past do-re-mi. They wonder why they stay stuck, and usually feel ashamed, living lives of quiet desperation. If you want to get a sense for what this feels like, sing softly to yourself seven times "do-re-mi" right now. Stuck in a loop, right? Those stuck in this stage may ask themselves as they lay their head on a pillow at night, "What is stopping me?" Well, I have the answer. What's coming to stop you is the next phase: the first interval.

This interval is also called the first difficulty, and as we ascend the musical scale, a rest or pause marks its spot. At the first interval, we face denying force: any difficulty, big or small, that pushes you to retreat or change course. Let's return to the paleo diet example. Ten days in, you feel great. Then your fave uncle invites you to a barbecue, and you can't resist the hot-off-the-grill hamburger buns he chars just so, so you surrender and bite down hard. "I'll start again tomorrow," you think, but you don't. Weeks after the screenplay idea, you may think, "Man, that was a great idea," but you're busy at work and as the idea slips through your fingers, away goes the dream.

For those who persist past the first difficulty, though, the next stage is fa-so-la. This phase is super amaze. In fa-so-la, we reap the rewards of surpassing the difficulties of denying force. It's that moment when the corner cupcake shop you dreamed of opening for years has lines around the block day after day. The local newspaper profiles you, and a steady, six-figure income rolls in. You provide a comfortable life for your family doing what you love. Impressed friends seek your counsel and advice. You did it. The vast majority of those who make it to fa-so-la stop there. Who can blame them, really? It's so easy to be seduced by success. For a select few, though, two stages await.

For those who push past fa-so-la, the second interval, also known as the Law of Impossibility, is up next. The second interval features a "dark night of the soul" moment, where striving for si-do appears quite literally impossible. Beethoven went deaf. Steve Jobs? Fired from the company he started. Abraham Lincoln lost countless elections and suffered from crippling depression. For many, moments like these spell the end of the success story. Ceasing to strive for success in the same arena, they return to do-re-mi in a new octave of life, focusing on personal relationships, for example, or new hobbies. Yet Beethoven composed many of his major works, including the 9th Symphony, in a state of near total deafness. Jobs returned to Apple to shape it into the most profitable company in America. Lincoln guided the country through civil war, becoming arguably the greatest president in history. Each man pushed past impossible odds to reach the next stage.

Si-do is the summit of success. Impossible mastery. The peak of self-actualization. Having transcended the second interval, lives lived at this level represent seemingly impossible levels of aptitude and excellence. In addition to success, philanthropy and community empowerment tend to be key features here. To return to our bakeshop example, si-do is the stage where the owner builds a highly profitable, socially conscious brand where for every cupcake sold, a hungry child in a neglected country receives a bowl of rice. In Plato's Allegory of the Cave, the man who saw that the impressions on the wall were the shadows of those living in light, then left the cave and returned to liberate his cave-dwelling comrades, lived in a state of si-do.

In fact, a divine being created us so that we could spend our lives striving for this state of completion. In the Book of Genesis, God creates the universe in six days, and rests on the seventh. His rest on the seventh day is a metaphorical way of saying, "Your turn to complete it!" It's as if this divine being is telling us, "Okay, I did all this. Now, you go!" We have been gifted a seventh day—one that spans our lifetime—to *dance with God*. In this sense, we have the power to co-create with the Divine. But we have to really reach for this consciousness if we want to make that long seventh day of creation really matter.

> We have been gifted a seventh day—one that spans our lifetime—to *dance with God*.

We're pretty terrible at reaching for God, though, which is why denying force keeps most people in do-re-mi their entire lives. In the famous image on the ceiling of the Sistine Chapel, God reaches down to touch the fingertip of Adam. The way Michelangelo painted it was to detail all the muscles in his chest straining. He reaches so hard! But Adam leans back lazily and simply can't be bothered to move the last digit of his index finger to touch the Divine.

In a nutshell, this is our dilemma. A benevolent energy desperately tries to connect with us, but we are too misguided and afraid to lift our fucking index finger, and have what we have always longed for! Personally, I don't believe God rested because he left humanity behind or he was exhausted. No, God rested to give us the opportunity to pull off a nearly impossible feat: to remember the Divine exists at all, and then reach out to touch it.

Live Above the Law of Seven

To live above the Law of Seven, start by recalling the two axes of reality that govern our being. The first is horizontal—the tangible, external realities we face in the physical world. The quest for success on this plane entails key components. Diligence. Relentlessness. Resilience. Networks of allies, champions, and mentors. Some reach worldly success on this level without ever taking a moment to meditate.

But *the ability to actually enjoy success* requires intensive work along a second axis—the vertical. This plane is the invisible, spiritual dimension of meditation, prayer, and deep fulfillment—the substance and texture of this book. It is when we live our lives at the intersection of these axes that our lives explode with material success *and* deep, enduring happiness. In other words, you really can have it all. The catch is, all that's required is long-term, continuous, intensive effort along both lines.

> It is when we live our lives at the intersection of these axes that our lives explode with material success *and* deep, enduring happiness.

Verification Point

Locate an area of your life where you have a dream, goal, or vision that you seek to shepherd to a state of successful completion. Identify the notes you're currently playing on the scale. Are you in do-re-mi? First interval? Fa-so-la? Ask yourself where you've given in to denying force, and what will be required of you to move up the scale.

Use the horizontal line to cultivate a community, refine your plans, and take concrete actions; use the vertical line to cultivate calm, bliss, and joy. Though the process may take months, years, or decades, it can feel easy and light as a feather due to your work along the vertical line. Shirk neither axis, and move forward patiently a day at a time.

In your journal, using the goal you identified above, write about the phase of the scale you're currently in. Why are you in this stage? Where are opportunities to move forward? Next, describe what it feels like to reach si-do with this goal. Use the present tense to write about this state as if it's already occurred. Be expansive in your thinking, dream big, and write descriptively.

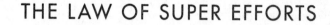

10

THE LAW OF SUPER EFFORTS

So, how do you push past denying force and impossibility to reach your aim? Well, it requires massive energy, will, and force—what I call a super effort. The concept is sort of like those moments of superhuman strength where a man lifts a car to free a trapped child, or a mom manages to fight off an attacking polar bear to protect her kids. But you don't need to be attacked by a bear or get trapped under a car to utilize super effort! In fact, you can use it for trials large or small—whenever you feel like you've hit a wall in your spiritual practice, or with any goal or desire you have.

At times, you move through life with ease. No need for super efforts! Blue skies, balmy temps, serenity. Life rolls in ebbs and flows, and sometimes you're just riding a wave, blissed out and stress-free. In do-re-mi, you're thrilled about a new project. Floating through fa-so-la, you have loads of evidence all around you that everything's working just fine. At the summit of si-do, you're done; you've reached the goal.

Sometimes, though, you hit the wall of denying force—any

difficulty, big or small, that pushes you backwards. Your landscape may look bleak and meaningless, and you may face what feels like an existential threat. Or you may just not want to meditate and hit the gym when you wake up. You may feel angry that you've committed to a spiritual practice. In fact, aggravation is a good indicator of the need for a super effort. For some, weather or distance may require a super effort to keep a commitment. The addict will need a super effort to get sober. I sure did!

So, how do we create super efforts? A super effort is doing the thing you don't want to do. It's an opposite action. To generate a super effort, several strategies succeed. Pause and sit. Breathe deeply into your diaphragm, and ask for the will to match your actions to the person you say you want to be. Scream into a pillow. Put yourself on a clock, and call a trusted friend to vent for two minutes. Get down on your hands and knees and ask the universe for energy and strength. Take a cold shower. A super effort is like a booster shot, designed to be temporary and used as needed. Super efforts pay out in multiples, too. When you do what you really don't want to do, you double the pleasure of the reward when you're done.

> A super effort is doing the thing you don't want to do.

A few key points. I'm not just describing willpower. In order to generate a super effort, we're looking to gin up massive energy from the vertical line. So, at the same time that you work with all your might, lean back and trust that this vertical line will run the energy through you. In other words, mixed with your actions, a super effort is something you can rest in the hands of God to will.

Super efforts can be financial, too. Last year, a few friends referred a young woman—deeply stuck and distraught over a nasty breakup—to me as a client. Unable to pay my rate at first, she later resolved to pay for several months of sessions by any means, seeing our work as vital. In other words, she made a super effort. After I worked with her for six weeks, she was ready to meet with her ex, and set up a coffee date. Unimpressed with him by this point, she processed the relationship healthily, let go of the ex, and set herself free to date again. Her super effort enabled her to heal and move on.

Live Above the Law of Super Efforts

In order to live above the Law of Super Efforts, be the constant, not the variable. In other words, keep your commitments and don't succumb to the desire to skip regimented work. Don't feel like meditating when you wake up tired and groggy? Ask for energy, willingness, and strength. Start to make decisions based on your commitments, rather than how you feel at a given moment. In other words, fuck your feelings! They're not going to help you when it comes to marshaling the strength required for a super effort. You know the voice in your head that says, "Oh I just don't want to" or "I don't feel like it"? That's denying force talking, and it's meaningless from now on. It's dead to you. You may not want to do the work to get a beach body, learn to balance a bank account, or figure out how the fuck to be a good mom or dad. But there are times in life when you need to level up. Those times require super efforts.

Verification Point

Recognize that denying force may sound like you and talk like you, but it's not you. The reason you feel shameful and shitty when you give in to this impulse is you know you've succumbed to something that isn't you. So, install a new mantra to respond to moments of denying force: "No, I will not be replaced by this lower version of myself. I remain convinced that I am who I say I am."

11

THE LAW OF "SHOULDS"

S top "shoulding" all over yourself!

So much of what we do, think, say, and believe flows from a flawed sense of "'should." This sense stems from childhood, when we are taught sets of rules via the norms of society. Many of these rules—some of them legal ones—are necessary. They preserve order, keep people safe, and allow society to function. But many rules we follow are based entirely on false ideas we have accrued about the way we *should* behave, speak, and think. But really, who are we to say how things should or shouldn't be? Once we start to evaluate this system of "should," we often delight in a new sense of freedom.

When you're a kid, you learn valuable norms. Make your bed. Don't act wild and crazy in math class. Brush your teeth every day. Other "shoulds" are less helpful. I live in New York City, and some of my fellow New Yorkers think they shouldn't say hello, make eye contact with, or smile at strangers, especially on the subway. Why? There's really no reason, other than they've decided that's the way it should be. So, one crippling side effect of living under "should" for some New Yorkers can be a loss of connection. Typically, when we disconnect from our communities, we unplug from the divine—all in order to fit in, save face, and look good.

Can I get real with you for a sec? I have a curvy booty. As a teenager, my overly protective grandparents terrified me with horrifying stories about sex assaults, and so I wore billowy boy clothes, thinking I should hide my curves. To this day, I get self-conscious shaking my hips on a dance floor in a sexy outfit, or even when I want to have a solo dance party in my home! Once I began to study these laws, I woke up to this "should," and realized I was trapped by someone else's beliefs from years ago. After years of cultivating divided attention and conscious being, I had an epiphany. I realized that to live above this law I needed to don sexy, tight outfits and wear them in public. Terrifying at first, it's now a super-liberating practice, and I feel free from this "should."

> Can I get real with you for a sec? I have a curvy booty. As a teenager, my overly protective grandparents terrified me with horrifying stories about sex assaults, and so I wore billowy boy clothes.

Living under this law, when you speak or act, instead of speaking or acting on your own truth, you parrot sentiments you heard when you were five years old, and you're not even aware of it! "Shoulds" lead us to care too deeply what others think of us, and we spend thousands of hours of our precious lives making sure we're perceived just so. It's exhausting. In addition, you may question your choices constantly, wondering whether they conform to an imagined set of rules. You may also inflict your "shoulds" on others, making them feel shitty or put down.

Recently, I had a client who traveled to Miami constantly to spend time with her elderly parents. What a good daughter, right? The problem was, she had a high-powered career, a husband, *and* three children, and when she came to me, she complained that she felt like her frequent trips were erasing her from her own life. Overwhelmed and stressed, she persisted, racking up the frequent flyer miles.

What she didn't know at the time was this: her parents actually didn't need her to come all that often, and when she visited, she was so stressed out—conference calls, detailed instructions for care of the kids back home—that her parents couldn't really enjoy her, and had been secretly hoping she would visit *less* often. When I explained this law to her, she began to see that she was governed by a sense of obligation that didn't exist. As she scaled back her trips, she enjoyed her parents more, they enjoyed her more, and she didn't have to leave her small children behind. Living above the law, she designed her life in a way that brought her immense satisfaction.

Live Above the Law of "Shoulds"

Notice when you deny or restrict because of a "should" you picked up from a parent or teacher and have adopted as "the truth." Choose to live in curiosity about the norms and rules you live by. When making decisions, ask yourself, "Why am I choosing this way? Is this something I truly want, or am I doing this because I think I *should*?" When you lose these old ideas about how you should be, you become more childlike

> Choose to live in curiosity about the norms and rules you live by.

and innocent, no longer paralyzed or afraid. Think about how carefree little kids are! When you're not governed by "shoulds," you become freer, more childlike.

Above this law, you live an imaginative, risk-taking life. You may find yourself singing on a parade float or sneaking into a fancy restaurant. Maybe when you're in Paris, you'll run through the Louvre with friends to see

I'm not saying everyone's destiny is to be like the provocative street artist Banksy, but we all have a little Banksy in us.

who can get across the museum the fastest. I'm not saying everyone's destiny is to be like the provocative street artist Banksy, but we all have a little Banksy in us. Until we can subvert some of the rules, we'll never be able to make our lives unique and surprising, and live above this law.

Verification Point

After reading this chapter, notice when you obey rules that don't even exist. Are you living under someone else's "shoulds" in your day-to-day life? Instead, choose to practice childlike wonder. Pass by a rose? Literally stop and smell it. Want to pet someone's cute puppy? Go do that. If you happen to live in New York City, for god sakes, make eye contact and say hi to a stranger on the street! On another note, watch when you start "shoulding" on your partner, friends and family, or a colleague. Begin to question whether the rules you may seek to impose on others really matter, after all.

12

THE LAW OF MECHANICAL GOODNESS

Being mechanically good is kind of like being an angry robot. You hold a door open for a stranger, and wait irritably when he doesn't walk as quickly as you'd like. You jump up to do dishes while your family chitchats leisurely over dessert. Then you load the dishwasher, stewing in resentment: "I always have to do it all myself!" Under this law you act on autopilot, doing good deeds without reaping spiritual rewards. Of course, it's vital to serve others and perform acts of kindness! But to practice genuine goodness, we need to change the *way* we perform these acts, with conscious intention.

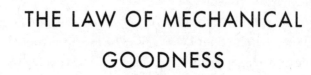

Being mechanically good is kind of like being an angry robot.

Mechanically powered, you have a near inability to say "no" to requests for favors, but when you find yourself in need of a favor, you look around and find no "yes" in sight. Robotically putting others' needs before your own, you're overwhelmed by your many mechanical kind acts. In this state, you become a kind of doormat, trampled by others and worn down by all your goodness. The worst part is, you're not even doing it consciously. In fact, under this law, you'll be unable *not* to act this way.

Mechanical goodness is skin deep, too. As we peel back the veneer of morality, we typically uncover resentment, negativity, or selfishness even *while* the mechanically good person is being kind. It makes sense, since this state is really the product of a whole lot of "shoulds." Locked into a cycle of doing for others, we say yes to too many requests, so this kind of formulaic kindness tends to foster a martyr complex, too. It's so confusing to those who suffer from this problem. They may wonder, "How can I be doing all this good and still feel like a victim?"

Let's return to the "I'm holding the door for you, so won't you please hurry up?" moment. You hold the door for a stranger, and wait expectantly. Unaware, he's looking down at his phone, which irritates you. He looks up, and sheepishly hustles toward the door to show you he appreciates the gesture. In this scenario, you're both trapped in the law of mechanical goodness. Stuck in what you think you *should* do, you sacrifice serenity to do a favor the guy doesn't necessarily even want or need. In this sense, mechanical goodness is akin to a kind of codependence.

Recently, I worked with a lonely client in her thirties with a sizable trust fund. Fresh off a divorce, she owned a spacious loft in Brooklyn, and usually let a broke friend, even broke friends of friends, couch surf in her home. Predictably, the couch surfers took her generosity for granted. They ate her food, left messes, and even stole her stuff. In turn, she resented them, but couldn't quite bring herself to kick them out. Lonely, she also slept with some of them. One guy stayed for five months!

As she meditated and asked every morning, and saw herself

through the lens of mechanical goodness, she realized she didn't actually care too much about saving her couch surfing crew from a life on the streets. In fact, she was kind of holding them hostage in her loft. Why? She was lonely, but hid from intimacy via her never-ending carousel of couch surfers. Over time, I worked with her to start dating again, and as she invited her dates over to her place, the hangers-on felt less and less comfy. Empowered, she set exit timelines, and they all left. As she formed a new relationship with solitude, she met a great guy with a home of his own. He didn't need her couch. They're together to this day.

Live Above the Law of Mechanical Goodness

In the Jewish faith, those who observe Hanukkah light eight candles, one on each night of the holiday. The ninth, the Shamash, is a helper or servant candle, used to light all the others. This candle illuminates the menorah and burns to light others. But it doesn't go out when it lights the other candles. It retains its light and energy. In acts of goodness, you're meant to be the Shamash. The crazy thing is, when you share light, it doesn't diminish your own. You have an endless supply to share! As you learn to share your light, you'll find that it is an unending supply. You are meant to give in a way that lights up the world around you, and lights you up, too. Any other giving is mechanical goodness.

So, when someone asks for a favor or you feel compelled to do "good," make intentional choices. In the midst of a kind act,

> The crazy thing is, when you share light, it doesn't diminish your own.

note what is driving you by asking questions. Are you being led by what you think is your duty? Or are you leading with love and a genuine desire to serve? Of course, you have real duties and tasks. But note how it feels when you consciously choose those acts, rather than treating them like a burden. Where mechanical goodness drains you, authentic goodness energizes and fills you with joy.

Verification Point

In order to verify mechanical goodness, practice saying "no" when you need to. It's a complete sentence! As you pray and meditate, ask for guidance to distinguish between genuine goodness and mechanical. Practice asking for help, and open yourself to receive support. When performing a "good" deed or favor for someone, observe your motive. Are you taking the action from a place of joy, because you want to make someone else happy? Or, is your goodness mechanical? Motive is everything. Unless you can see your motives clearly, you'll be under this law forever.

13

THE LAW OF NEGATIVE
EMOTIONS

The Buddha once said, "You throw swords—falling in my silence they become flowers." Sounds peaceful, right? Sometimes, though, you're too busy throwing swords to stay silent. Upset by what someone says, you lash out. Threatened, you say cruel or nasty words hurting ones you love. Words really can cut like swords, can't they? It doesn't *have* to be this way, though. Above this law, silence is golden. In fact, using a simple toolkit, you can learn to hold your tongue *and* transmute being upset with others into a deep, pure calm. In other words, you can turn swords into flowers.

How do you practice this kind of calm? See that you sometimes do hold ill will toward others. It's true. You do! You're also going to have to admit that when you yell at someone, or get cruel, it hurts him *and* you. This can be a bit of a stretch for some; it can be so easy to justify what we do or say. "Well, I'm *right* anyway" you may think, or "It felt good to get that out."

Also, "He deserved it." As long as you wield nasty emotions as a net positive in your life, you won't be willing to stop. If that's the case, ask for willingness to set aside the old mind-set and try on a new one.

Really, though: would you rather be happy or right? If you choose happy, the first work is to simply observe when you fly off the handle. That's it! It sounds weird, but initially you don't need to try to stop saying fucked-up things to the ones you love. Just observe when you do. This is actually great news, since you can't just force quit emotional instincts. So, what *can* you do? Well, you need a tool to slow down runaway emotions, and that's where meditation comes into play.

When you cultivate a meditative state, you can almost slow down time, spot a negative emotion from miles away, and bat it away with ease. To be clear, I'm not saying you won't ever feel angry, vindictive, or resentful. What I *am* saying is you can create a kind of lag time and put your emotions on slo-mo. Visualize what I'm saying via a famous moment in *The Matrix*: in the hero Neo's early stages of consciousness training inside a computer simulation, he slows down bullets shot at him to a slow speed where he can see them coming, then dodge. Bullets. Swords. It's really all the same, isn't it?

> When you cultivate a meditative state, you can almost slow down time, spot a negative emotion from miles away, and bat it away with ease.

To put the same kind of space between you and unpleasant emotions, a daily practice is vital. When you meditate regularly, you put deposits of calm and stillness into a kind of spiritual reserve you can draw on in an upset moment. *In* that moment, too, breathe in through the nose and let your breath expand to hit the

◇◇◇◇◇◇◇◇◇◇◇◇◇◇◇◇◇◇◇◇◇◇◇◇◇◇

When you meditate regularly, you put deposits of calm and stillness into a kind of spiritual reserve you can draw on in an upset moment.

◇◇◇◇◇◇◇◇◇◇◇◇◇◇◇◇◇◇◇◇◇◇◇◇◇◇

ribs. Silently repeat a calming mantra or prayer in real time, even as you sit across from a colleague, client, or kid. Ask, "Thy will be done." Or simply change the topic. Using these tools, you'll be able to disappear tidal waves of emotion so they don't crash into you and splash others.

Several years ago, I worked with a client who lived in Brooklyn. For the uninitiated, taxis used to hate to cross the bridge from Manhattan to the borough. Low fare. An empty car on the trip back. Maybe a sketchy neighborhood. You get the picture. So, every time a cab driver refused her, and it happened quite a bit, she yelled. She screamed. She kicked the door. She threatened to call the Taxi and Limousine Commission. She whined that she was right, since after all, it is illegal. She was right, but it got her nowhere.

As I taught her to live above negative emotions, she started to use the toolkit I laid out above. She breathed, meditated, asked for compassion, and an amazing thing happened. Sitting halfway into the backseat of a cab, the driver briskly said "No," and she had a breakthrough. As she breathed, paused, and prayed, in her conscious state an image of his life popped into her mind.

Through his eyes, she saw a wife, kids, and a family at home he worked sixteen hours a day to support. She saw a boss who called him and told him to be back in ten minutes or he'd be fired. Calm now, she thanked him for his time, got out, and hailed another cab. In that moment, she lived above negative emotions. She didn't know him at all. Who knows if the story she intuited was true? But she interpreted the moment charitably, and preserved a still calm in her soul. As she started to live above negative emotions, in fact, she easily got cabbies to take her home to Brooklyn. She never had the problem again.

Live Above the Law of Negative Emotions

To live above this law, start to act like you're in love. I mean it! A life lived consciously is a lot like being in love. C'mon, in that blissed-out state does anything really bother you? Let's say a flash rainstorm one night destroys your favorite loafers. In your normal state, you're livid. You might be pissed at clouds for weeks! But if you're out on the town with a woman you've just fallen in love with and the same flash storm hits, do you really give a shit about loafers? You'd probably go sing in the rain together. You're in love! You're in an altered state of being.

The goal is to alter your everyday state to match the "I'm in love" one. I know, I know. You're skeptical. But it *is* possible. I know, because I live it! Seriously, ask my husband. So many days, a few hours in, I'll exclaim, "This is the best day of my life!" He usually laughs, because it'll be a random Tuesday and I have no new reason to be so happy, other than the fact that I'm alive. But I work hard for it. So, do the same. Remember that everyone you meet is fighting a battle you know nothing about. So be kind. Always. Apply your whole being to the tools I've laid out, and you'll start to live above the Law of Negative Emotions.

Verification Point

The next time you want to yell, scream, or get nasty, ask for stillness to pause. Step outside if you need to, and grab some fresh air. Ask your higher power for compassion and empathy, and to see the issue or situation from a new point of view. In terms of the person you're upset with, say, "Please show me where he's coming from. Give me compassion, and shape me into the person You want me to be."

If you couldn't pause and instead lashed out, divide your attention and observe yourself while you yell at your brother, bark at a cabdriver, or say something nasty to your wife. It's pretty gross. Believe me. I've done it myself! But being aware is the first step, and once you watch yourself act this way many times, you'll hopefully get sick of it enough that you'll stop, or at least become willing to pause and ask for help.

14

THE LAW OF BUFFERS

I like to ask my clients, "How much joy can you stand?" Seems like an easy question. You may say, "I can stand *all* the joy!" But you may also change your tune when I show you how you try to mediate, or lessen the shock of bliss all the time. In other words, you buffer it. Buffers are simply habits and practices we use to avoid the totality of consciousness. We buffer not only bliss, but also sadness and pain—really *any* feeling that allows us to experience ourselves completely. In this state, we not only fail to avoid pain, we dull joy, too. So, how do we learn to make ourselves available to experience the full range of human emotions?

Well, first we have to see how we buffer reality. We procrastinate to buffer the brevity of life, pretending we have all the time in the world. We feign apathy toward unrealized dreams, calling them unrealistic to buffer the pain of unfulfilled desires. We toss sarcastic comments into intimate moments with

> We procrastinate to buffer the brevity of life, pretending we have all the time in the world.

friends or loved ones to buffer vulnerability. We rationalize away feedback from others to buffer the pain of growing and changing, choosing instead to stay in our comfort zone.

It's ironic that we try so hard to buffer reality, because what awaits us on the other side of buffers is bliss—the serene, calm contentment that comes from a willingness to open ourselves to the present moment. In a way, we often see our most vulnerable feelings like a frog: ugly, wet, and yucky. Meditation and asking empowers you to embrace tenderness, break beyond buffers, and kiss the frog, entangling yourself with its messy sliminess. When we do that, to our delight, the frog is actually a prince. As we find the fearlessness to embrace vulnerability in our lives, our buffers tend to slip away.

◇◇◇◇◇◇◇◇◇◇◇◇◇◇◇◇◇◇◇◇◇◇◇◇◇◇◇◇◇

Meditation and asking empowers you to embrace tenderness, break beyond buffers, and kiss the frog, entangling yourself with its messy sliminess. When we do that, to our delight, the frog is actually a prince.

◇◇◇◇◇◇◇◇◇◇◇◇◇◇◇◇◇◇◇◇◇◇◇◇◇◇◇◇◇

I had a client who buffered a deep desire to change the world via the written word. Though her dream was to write political exposés for *The New York Times*, she took a job with a fashion magazine, afraid of the messy intensity and egos of political reporting. Here, she buffered with indecision and avoidance. Though she also wanted to write a novel for ten years, she never made more than a start, buffering her dream via procrastination. In our sessions together, I taught her the concept of buffers, and showed her how she had been deploying them to protect herself from a fear of failure.

Not surprisingly, when she got clear about how she had been buffering in her life, she immediately, unconsciously, found a new way to buffer reality. She dove deep into shame around how she had, from her point of view, "wasted" ten years avoiding her calling. Sans our work together, she may have wasted the next ten years too in a buffering spiral. When I pointed out she was just using a new tool to buffer, though, she broke down in a moment of clarity, seeing that buffers are kind of like that whack-a-mole game at old amusement parks. Until you disintegrate the root cause of your need to buffer reality itself, another mole is going to pop up that you need to whack. Finally after ten long years, she's hundreds of pages in on a first draft!

Live Above the Law of Buffers

To live above this law, you need to begin to shed your buffers, but there's a catch. The tricky thing about buffers is you can't shed them all at once. A friend of mine speculated that those in psychotic states were, on some level, people whose buffers had been stripped away all at once. You can't try to give up all your buffers, as the shedding of all these defenses at the same time would let in so much light at once it would be akin to staring directly into the sun. You wouldn't want to do that, right? We need to choose those buffers affecting us most acutely, and strive to shed them one at a time. It's like peeling an onion layer by layer, slowly over time.

How do we disintegrate the root cause of all our attempts to buffer reality? One way to start to address this challenge is to ask yourself the question I mentioned at the top of this chapter: how much joy can you stand? The root cause of all buffers is resistance to a state of bliss, as the pathway to bliss runs *through* unpleasant feelings, not the routes we try to run around them. Ask to be open to all feelings pouring through you at any moment. After morning meditation, ask for clarity around ways you buffer, and the courage to let these go, then move boldly through the uncomfortable growth that's required to reach awakened joy.

Verification Point

Since you can only remove one buffer at a time, choose one you're using to keep yourself asleep, like gossip, sarcasm, or complaining. For the next thirty days, don't use that buffer. If you choose complaining, for example, don't complain for thirty days. You can even program a once-a-day reminder into your phone: "No Buffers!" When you do complain, bite your lip. You may end up with a very sore lip by the end of the month, but you'll also see what a beautiful life awaits you free from your buffers!

15

THE LAW OF LEAKS

What happens when you drop a grain of sand into a gas tank? Well, nothing, of course. Drop in ten grains, still no problem. But over time, if you funnel several thousand grains of sand into the tank, the car won't drive. In the same way, when you block the entry to the soul with small lies, habitual lateness, worries, or petty jealousies, over time its workings grind to a halt and you leak spiritual energy. Every day we awaken with a certain amount of energy given to us to connect to the soul and realize our ambitions and dreams. Often, we don't use the energy for those aims, though. Instead, we leak it. So, let's find the leaks that trouble you, close them, and retain the energy you need to manifest your optimal self.

> Living a spiritual life on planet earth is kind of like riding down an escalator. With no effort, you go down.

Living a spiritual life on planet earth is kind of like riding down an escalator. With no effort, you go down. In the same way, without any spiritual effort, we leak energy all over the place. Sans spiritual effort on our part, we consistently make choices unaligned with our aim, leaving us uneasy and dissatisfied. When we feel overly drained at the end of a day, it's often a product of leaks. Subconsciously, we may realize that when we preserve energy, the universe calls us to action, which makes us acutely aware that we're responsible for our destiny. Shying away from this responsibility, we arrive late to important meetings, gossip, and self-sabotage in other ways. Riding down an escalator is just about the easiest thing you can do.

Lies pose a key threat, as even the smallest mistruths leak energy. Now look, research suggests the average adult lies at least once a day, so I get it. Exaggerating a résumé. Saying you've read a book you haven't. Cheating on your partner or your taxes. In terms of leaks, it matters not if anyone else clocks your dishonesty. The problem is *you* know, and the knowledge robs you of your peace of mind. Sometimes, the accumulation of small and big lies over years and decades creates a kind of skewed set of perceptions that we actually begin to see as reality.

One way we leak energy is by failing to keep commitments. We may arrive late to appointments, leading others to worry. We may cancel at the last minute because we "just don't feel like it." These problems play out when we make decisions based on our feelings rather than our commitments. Making choices based on how we feel keeps pending decisions on our mind, and leads us to worry and stress about items we could process and eliminate quickly. When we choose from a place of commitment to our aims, however, our energy and power increase.

Several years ago, I had a client who was leaking via paranoia, often wasting time going through her boyfriend's phone looking for reasons to be jealous. Though she never found any proof, she accused him of cheating on her, even though, based on all available evidence, he wasn't. When I showed her that she was leaking energy via this obsession, she began to see that jealousy was distracting her from her life, generally, and drained vitality from the relationship. She realized that it was indicative of an inability to trust, and she made a commitment to stop unlocking his phone.

Once she sealed the leak, trust returned, and because her boyfriend felt trusted, he became more open and vulnerable, and they grew happier and more intimate. Just as important, she was able to direct the energy she had been spending on a jealous obsession toward her true ambitions. She began to eat healthier, worked out more often, and started the paperwork to form the nonprofit she had long dreamed of starting. Closing off the leak opened space in her life for health, a clear understanding of her purpose, and the flow state she lives in to this day.

Live Above the Law of Leaks

How do we learn to stop leaks? First, begin to take notice of where your words don't match your actions. Observe even the smallest lie or half-truth, and strive to practice clarity and honesty in every moment. If you struggle with indecisiveness, be decisive, trusting that the practice will power the primary aim. If you can complete a task, do it immediately. Make your bed. Answer the quick email right now. Procrastination puts unnecessary worries in the mind and clogs our thoughts. We want a mind like water that channels our lives in service of others. As we start to close off leaks, we gain the ability to direct the energy we've preserved in the service of our primary aim.

In your meditation, notice the leaks that are most prominent in your life. Notice how worries, fears, and anxieties multiply when we leak via indecision, dishonesty, and noncommittal ways of being. Observe how much energy you may leak when you move into regret or ruminate on past decisions. If you are often late, ask to be transformed to a human who arrives early for all occasions. If you tend into exaggerate or speak half-truths, ask to become honest at all moments. Use the tool of asking and request to have your key leaks sealed in the areas that pose the biggest problems to you.

Verification Point

In order to verify the Law of Leaks, look at the ways you leak—white lies, lateness, gossip, whatever—and ask God to remove the one that causes you the most trouble. Then, take opposite action for the next ninety days. Research suggests that it takes around ninety days to form a new habit, and this method will transform your habitual practices *if* you commit to it. For example, you can commit to being early to every single appointment, meeting, and gathering on your calendar for the next ninety days. Use your journal, too, to note how many times you leak in a given week. At the end of the week, review your actions and ask again for the Divine to remove troublesome, recurring behaviors.

16

THE LAW OF INNER CONSIDERING

Can you read minds like Professor X? If so, congrats! You can skip this chapter. For everyone else, inner considering—fixating on ourselves, especially on what we think others think about us—poses a significant spiritual challenge. This law sows self-doubt and insecurity as we obsessively try to guess and obsess about what others think of us. In this state, we react to others' postures, facial expressions, and moods, spinning out into resentment or jealousy based on little more than a single thought. Stuck in thoughts about ways we *think* others perceive us, we sometimes struggle socially or on social media, pulling back our unique self-expressions out of fear. Unless you're a mind-reading superhero, it's best to shy away from attempts at clairvoyance.

> Unless you're a mind-reading superhero, it's best to shy away from attempts at clairvoyance.

And yet. We still think we can discern others' motives and intent based on what we think. When we spend our time inner considering what others say and do, we react based on *what we think they think*, and usually try to manipulate outcomes based on this hall of mirrors we've built in our minds. Inner considering typically leads us to gossip, as well, because talking relieves the pressure and tension we've built up via the elaborate system of second-guessing in our minds.

Inner considering confronts us at nearly all moments in our lives. I've worked with wealthy clients paralyzed by shame, guessing others think they haven't earned it. The same has been true of clients with lesser means. They decline invitations and stay in, thinking that others will judge them for old clothes or an old car. If you're dating or in a relationship, you may keep a sexual fantasy secret because you're afraid your partner will judge you. You may want to wear that super-sexy outfit in your closet, but you're afraid of what others will say. Inner considering is any way you deprive the world of the gift of your authentic self.

Let's say you have a big decision to make, such as buying a home, getting married, or switching careers. In inner considering, you weigh pros and cons based on what you think others will think, leading you away from *your* aims. Acting from imagined future thoughts and words of others, you may shape an entire life around a whole host of make-believe voices and perspectives. Goethe once wrote, "Trying to please everybody is the most ridiculous of pretensions," and this pretense flows from inner considering. In this state, we diminish ourselves and shrink our soul's light in the world. It's a painful way to live.

I worked with a client for about a year whose mind was rife with inner considering. As she studied these laws and worked with me as a private student, we worked through several exercises and reviewed her history. She used divided attention to observe herself, asked God to reveal *her* truth, and revealed openly for the first time that she was gay. She told me she had known this truth on some level for years, but was afraid of what her family and friends would think of her, especially her mom and dad. Seeing the consequences of inner considering, she came out to her closest loved ones, and began to date women freely. Her parents embraced her decision to reveal *her* true sexuality with open arms.

Live Above the Law of Inner Considering

The trick to living above this law is to move from worry about what others think to thoughts of how you can serve them. Really listen in conversations, cultivating empathy for needs, concerns, and dreams. Ask lots of questions. Listen carefully to responses, so you can ask thoughtful follow-ups. Research suggests the latter practice is especially gratifying; we all need to be heard! Look for opportunities to serve others in your community: volunteer to cook at a soup kitchen, or give up your seat on a crowded train. Cultivate a sense for how it feels to receive food when hungry and penniless, or to be able to sit down on aching, tired legs. In other words, cultivate the art of *external* considering.

Some of you may say, "But I always think of others. That's my problem. I think of them too much, and I'm still unhappy." Or, you may be unfailingly polite, asking questions, but robotically. I totally hear you. If you're not experiencing the freedom and joy that flow from truly considering others' needs, your goodness is probably mechanical. Mechanical goodness is a buffer, and doesn't equal the empathy of external considering. For the mechanically good, a few practices are available. Notice that the reason you do for others is you're addicted to being needed. It's still all about *you*! So, stop helping others for a bit, and stop being a resentful servant. Maybe take some time to pamper yourself and see how it feels.

Verification Point

Be kind to everyone you meet today, and practice external considering. Ask questions and listen to others' wants and worries. Ask follow-up questions. Put yourself in their shoes, and think about *their* needs and desires. Practice these tools often, and observe the sense of peace and ease that flow in. Go out of your way to do random acts of kindness, especially when you don't feel like it. When you naturally think about yourself all the time, it is literally supernatural to authentically consider the needs of others.

17

THE LAW OF HOUSEHOLDING

Have you ever wanted to buy happiness? Well, I have good news! In a sense, you really can. With attentiveness to your finances, you can free yourself from the chaos of money worries and buy time to cultivate the joy of your soul. This is what it means to be a good house-holder. In the same way you can't build a house without a proper foundation, you can't build a spiritual life without taking care of the nuts and bolts of financial reality. In

◇◇◇◇◇◇◇◇◇◇◇◇◇◇◇◇◇◇◇◇◇◇◇◇◇◇◇◇

Have you ever wanted to buy happiness? Well, I have good news! In a sense, you really can.

◇◇◇◇◇◇◇◇◇◇◇◇◇◇◇◇◇◇◇◇◇◇◇◇◇◇◇◇

fact, the deft and stable management of money is a key component of running your own spiritual "house" effectively. Otherwise, you lack the time and resources to build a foundation for your soul here on earth.

You may say, "But I'm a dreamer! I don't want to think about *money*." Well, you're not the only one. I'm a dreamer, too! Of course, we want to dream big, but it's important that while we do so, our feet are planted on firm financial footing. Often, though, those of us who dream big think paying close attention to financial numbers is tacky or unspiritual. We want to live a fulfilling spiritual life, but we may shrink from the somewhat boring, mundane realities of daily life, thinking them unimportant. The work I study proposes that nothing could be further from the truth. In many ways, attentiveness to our finances is actually the foundation of an active spiritual life.

A stereotypical image of a spiritual seeker is that she has to renounce worldly possessions, live apart from society, and thrive in nature. I call bullshit. We are here on earth living a human life for a reason, and we're *meant* to engage with day-to-day living. Part of this life requires us to make a living and live a life grounded in reality. You can't nurture your soul if you're scrambling to pay bills, for example, as you can't focus on your primary aim. Ineffective householders also impose costs on others, borrowing money from friends, for example, or not paying for insurance, and irresponsibly shifting crippling debt to family in an accident.

> A stereotypical image of a spiritual seeker is that she has to renounce worldly possessions, live apart from society, and thrive in nature. I call bullshit.

Remember the vertical and horizontal lines of reality that form a cross? The horizontal plane expresses the tangible, external realities we face in the physical world, while the vertical line is the spiritual plane of reality, the world of the soul. Recall that our goal here on planet earth is to live at the intersection of these lines, both materially stable and grounded in the physical world and spiritually fulfilled in a prayerful, meditative practice. Householding tethers us to a responsible way of life on the hor-

izontal plane, freeing us to
spend energy and attention
to fulfillment along the vertical line.

On the horizontal line,
one of the most effective ways
to transform your relationship with money is through

◇◇◇◇◇◇◇◇◇◇◇◇◇◇◇◇◇◇◇◇◇◇

Householding tethers us to a
responsible way of life on the
horizontal plane, freeing us to
spend energy and attention to
fulfillment along the vertical line.

◇◇◇◇◇◇◇◇◇◇◇◇◇◇◇◇◇◇◇◇◇◇

affirmations, extraordinarily effective tools for shifting deeply held beliefs in all areas of our lives. You can practice affirmations in both written and verbal fashion. Looking at yourself in the mirror, you may say out loud ten times in a row, "I love money and money loves me." Or, "I am responsible with money." You may also choose to write an affirmation five to ten times in the morning for a week or two, drilling a new belief deep into your unconscious.

Until about seven years ago, I was just about the worst house-holder of all time. I often had to decline dinners, vacations, and concerts because I couldn't afford them. Sometimes, my friends would pay so I could join, but either way I felt ashamed. I also felt like a victim of circumstance. "I'm so bad at the basics of life," I thought, "maybe I should just leave it all behind." So, in an effort to escape my responsibilities as a householder, I moved to a literal ashram in upstate New York. Then I discovered responsi-bilities exist even on ashrams! I left after a week.

The point is, you can't escape householding. In order to change, I had to confront the fact that ambiguity and vagueness around money was a key problem. I began to track my income and expenses down to the penny, as clarity around finances is an essential first step to becoming an effective householder. As I gained clarity, I began to grasp how much it cost to live the life I desired. Understanding my own intrinsic value, my rates sky-

As I gained clarity, I began to grasp how much it cost to live the life I desired.

rocketed, and I started to feel as much joy spending money as I did earning it. I even liked paying my bills! I had become a prosperous householder.

Live Above the Law of Householding

Realize that conducting your financial affairs in a responsible, prosperous way is just as important as your quest to wake up spiritually. This is vital. Keep your commitments, do what you say you're going to do, and build value and trust in your word. If you're not a good householder, it's just about impossible to pursue a spiritual awakening, as you'll be too stressed out worrying about bills, taxes, or rent.

Pay conscious attention to what you need to support the earthly journey, as well as the spiritual one, and create the worldly prosperity you need to structure your spiritual life. If you can't pay your electrical bill, you need to stop fooling yourself. Sans effective householding, you're not going to awaken counting mala beads and burning sage in your bedroom. For some of you, a discovery of how to pay your electric bill on time every month might just be the most spiritual thing you've ever done.

For some of you, a discovery of how to pay your electric bill on time every month might just be the most spiritual thing you've ever done.

Verification Point

For this verification, let's look at your finances. Track your expenses and income for thirty days down to the penny. These days, there are so many apps for this, it's easy-peasy. At the end of this time period, examine your earning and spending, and then ask yourself, "Am I earning enough to support my lifestyle?" If the answer is no, avail yourself of the many tools out there to become more financially responsible. Use resources online to learn about spending plans, savings tools, and investing. Learn how to ask for a raise. Find a group of peers committed to building and preserving wealth. As you take all these actions, say an affirmation: "I am on my way to easily being able to afford anything I want."

18

THE LAW OF THE ABCS
OF INFLUENCE

Several years ago, I came across a powerful spiritual maxim. It's been attributed to Confucius, American Indians, and Rabbi Hillel the Elder, so if you actually know where it comes from, let me know! It goes like this:

> Mind your thoughts, for they become your words; mind your words, for they become your actions. Mind your actions, for they become your habits. Mind your habits, for they become your character. Mind your character, for it will become your destiny.

Sounds true, right? But how do you mind your thoughts? Well, one way is to pay attention to the influences that shape them. These influences are all around us, guiding our thought patterns and ways we perceive reality. From Facebook videos to the Bhagavad Gita, these influences shape our consciousness, for better or worse. In the work I teach, they break down across three levels: A, B, and C.

A level influence consists of trashy, cheap information. A is the lowest level of influence and easiest to consume. Think of simple, fun, cheap thrills like *Star* magazine and *Keeping Up with the Kardashians*. Most blockbuster films. It's easy influence that allows you not to have to think that hard. The values of A level influence often revolve around gossip, lying, vanity, and extreme image consciousness. These actions and values make it difficult for the soul to reveal itself, as the soul is vulnerable, sensitive, and somewhat raw. Overexposure to this level of influence closes the soul, as it's innocent and won't feel safe in these environments.

One step up, level B influences simplify high wisdom, wrap it in pop culture elements, and make it easier and more pleasant to digest. Oprah. *Eat Pray Love*. Hot yoga. These inputs are influenced by divine consciousness, but because they mediate wisdom with fun elements, they mimic universal truths, but do not hold them purely. To quote Mary Poppins, under B influence, "a spoonful of sugar makes the medicine go down." While A influences can be harmful in high doses, B influences generally inspire and uplift. Yet these inputs tend to leave us wanting more, yearning for the universal wisdom we can only taste at this level.

C level influences express the highest form of information: knowledge directly communicated to us via the Divine. Ancient spiritual texts like the Torah, Bible, or Bhagavad Gita. Philosophers such as Marcus Aurelius and poets like Rumi. Painters like Rembrandt. Bach. Mozart. Typically, this level of influence requires time to process and digest, usually via repeated study and learning. C level influence is difficult to access, yet it serves as a channel for consciousness to flow directly into our souls. Our ability to gain deep, conscious insight generally requires a teacher or guide, who can help illuminate the wisdom and meaning in higher influences. This wisdom can even be contagious, especially when the presence of a teacher spreads level C influence to others.

> C level influence is difficult to access, yet it serves as a channel for consciousness to flow directly into our souls.

When I was twenty, I shaved my head, toured the country singing country folk songs in bars and clubs, then launched a pop culture detox in a quest to nourish my soul. Super-broke at the time, and squatting in Bushwick, Brooklyn, in what we now call a food desert, I switched from 69 cent ramen cups to brown rice, from pizza to the cheap plantains and tomatoes I could find at the bodega. I cooked on a hot plate in an abandoned building. I listened only to jazz and classical music, and watched only highbrow films at a Manhattan cinema house. When I emerged from my detox several years later and listened to a Jay-Z song, I deeply enjoyed it, realizing I had formed a new, healthier relationship with pop culture, one that didn't harm me.

Why leave any room for A influence at all? Let's be real. I like to read trashy magazines sometimes. That's just fine. Before I spent what feels like half my life in airplanes, fear used to kick in during takeoffs and landings. So I'd eat some junk food and grab an issue of *OK!* off the newsstand to distract myself. Other times, after a long and stressful day, I might want to come home and mindlessly binge Netflix for a couple hours. I'm human. It's all good. The point is to limit these influences to a contained part of our lives so they don't goad us to believe that the air-brushed pages of a glossy magazine have anything to do with reality.

Live Above the Law of the ABCs of Influence

A key point around this law is that you don't need to live a monastic life to be conscious. You don't need to go full detox. However, you can devote your energies to live more in C influence. A rough intake might look something like this: 60 percent of your time in B influence, 30 percent in C influence, and 10 percent in A influence. You'll probably spend most of your life taking in B influences, as these are both touched with divine wisdom and accessible to all. Eventually, you'll be able to tolerate higher doses of C influence, but this is a good starting point.

> A key point around this law is that you don't need to live a monastic life to be conscious.

So, notice how often you spend time indulging in A influence. Is it a lot? No problem at all! As sober alcoholics like to say, the first step on a path to change is admitting you have a problem, and the journey of a thousand miles begins with the first step. Even though it's uncomfortable and may be difficult at first, strive to make sure that the ratio of your exposure to A, B, and C forms of influence is healthy, and roughly follows the breakdown above. You can think of it in some ways like eating healthy. Generally speaking, if you want to be physically lean and fit, go easy on the carbs, eat lean protein, and dial up the fresh veggies and vegetable dishes. It's all about balance.

Verification Point

The German philosopher Schopenhauer once wrote, "Treat a work of art like a prince: let it speak to you first." In order to take in C influence, go to a museum and get silent in front of a beautiful painting, a masterpiece. Gaze at it for twenty to thirty minutes. Notice how much resistance kicks up, how hard it is. It's akin to that moment in the Bible when Moses can't look directly at God. His presence is that powerful. Exposing yourself to this level of influence for a sustained period can almost feel painful, but it's only by going through that pain that we're able to get into bliss.

> In order to take in C influence, go to a museum and get silent in front of a beautiful painting, a masterpiece.

19

THE LAW OF ACCIDENT

For all the loss I had experienced throughout my life, nothing compared to losing my daughter to SIDS when she was just four months old. The grief felt like too much to face head-on, so instead, I turned back to heroin to shut out the noise. On one of the rare nights when I made it out of my house to a party in Williamsburg, I got a phone call that the home I'd lived in for fourteen years in Jackson Heights, Queens, had caught on fire. Not coincidentally, my father—who lived above the Law of Accident—had moved out two weeks earlier.

I came home to find half my house was a dilapidated waste-land, charred and black. I continued to live there anyway, despite the fact that it still smelled like fire, and the only rooms left were the living room, a bedroom, and bathroom. I spent my time in this burned-down house either high or looking to get high. The only thing I really remember from that time, aside from the charred house, is that my drug dealer magically appeared to drop off more heroin.

The house burning down had nothing to do with any one

thing I did, but it did have to do with me being off my path. The Law of Accident was attempting to give me the opportunity to wake the fuck up. Of course, my case was extreme, in large part because I had wandered far from my intended path and purpose. In fact, the Law of Accident arrives in your life to alert you to the fact you've fallen asleep at the wheel. "Wake up!" it says as it gives you a nudge. "You're veering out of your lane."

It can also alert you, in subtle ways, that you're not tuned into your internal guidance system. Under the Law of Accident, you only sort of kind of like your friends. At every party, you feel like you're at the "wrong table."

> At every party, you feel like you're at the "wrong table."

You see a fabulous guy or girl walk by with your favorite haircut, coat, and boots and you think "Wait, that's my life!" Then you look at yourself in the mirror and you're dressed all wrong. You're at a job you hate, or you feel bored when you have a day off. It's like you fell into a life that's not yours by mistake. And you're right; it's not your life. It's an accident.

Last year, I worked with a client who desperately wanted to fall in love, to the point where he would date anyone. Not surprisingly, he found himself with people he didn't belong. He allowed himself to just fall into these situations. In his case, women were choosing him because he wasn't using his power to make his own choices. I told him love would never work out while he was living under this law. After all, to find true love, it's imperative to be living our own story and walking our own path. If we're not, how good or strong can that love really be? When you don't decide what you're looking for in life, life will give you accidents to wake you up. If you're not making choices as a conscious co-creator, you'll live under this law, prone to accident.

As he contemplated how this law appeared in his life, my

client was finally able to see that he was just giving himself away and landing in accidental situations. Once he realized this, he made an agreement with himself that when he *did* meet someone who fit the bill, he wouldn't sleep with her for ninety days. Instead, he was intentional, aware, and *present* in his interactions. He showed up for his own story, so he was able to discern when a situation was right or wrong. With this new awareness, he was able to act with intention and, within a year, met the woman who is now his wife. Because of his newfound presence, when he finally did meet her, he was acutely aware that she was the person for him.

Live Above the Law of Accident

Use your life as a wake-up call to ask, "What looks like an accident here?" Sort out the parts of your life you designed and the ones that came via accident. You can look at your career, partner, or health, for example. Is that really the career of your dreams, or did you just kind of fall into it? Did you choose to gain five pounds, or did it just kind of happen? Observe how much energy is wasted and time sucked when you're not consciously choosing the life you want. Start to get fed up with it, sick of it even. To verify that this law is above you is to see how it's wasting your life away.

> Did you choose to gain five pounds, or did it just kind of happen?

Above this law, though, you live the life of your dreams. It all feels intentional, like you designed it yourself. You experience gratitude as a verb, in perpetual awe at the life you built. At every party, you feel like you're at the "right table." You see a fabulous guy or girl with your favorite haircut, coat, and boots and remember you're looking in the mirror. You love your work so much it hurts to leave it. Your life is filled with travel and adventure. It's like you authored a life that's actually yours. And you're right. It is your life. By design.

Verification Point

Select an area of life where you see you're living under accident. An area you can truly and clearly say, "I did not intend this!" It could be a relationship, a job, or your weight. It's your choice. In your journal, write a clear, detailed, one-page vision for this area of your life, as if you knew you could get exactly what you wanted and there was no way you could fail. Ask, or pray, to set aside your old ideas. Ask, too, for new ones. Use your vision as a blueprint, and go build the life you want!

20

THE LAW OF SELF-WILL

I used to steal. Like, a lot. Occupational hazard of the junkie, I suppose. Coffee. Christmas ornaments. Kitchenware. Clothes. If it wasn't nailed down, I stole it. Trapped under this law, I schemed and stole to get what I wanted, but I was never satisfied. In other words, I didn't know the Law of Self-Will, which tells us that a life lived only to get what you want is empty. Under this law, you have one agenda: get, hold on to, have. Happily, though, to live above this law in divine will, you don't need to scrap that agenda. You just need to get for a new reason: to give.

So in self-will, we tend to try to get and have. Kids. Cars. Casas. Careers. Nothing wrong with any of that! In fact, self-will is good insofar as it leads us to make babies, achieve goals, and create prosperity. The problem in self-will is the motive. Under this law, you try to manipulate life to get what you want, thinking it will make you happy. But when you seek to realize life goals for their own sake, and then get them, you still feel dissatisfied. On to the next one, you think, "Oh, this one is *definitely* going to bring me peace and joy." Still, you're dissatisfied. A vicious cycle. The problem has nothing to do with the objects of our desire; it's our motives and means that cause us trouble.

God created in us the desire to "get" for ourselves and it does bring us pleasure, but that's only part of the process. To reach fulfillment, we need to "get to give," which is close to the meaning of the Hebrew word *kabbalah*, roughly translated as "receive in order to give." Using this approach to getting and giving, we live in divine will. Through this force we use our gifts, gets, and goals to serve others, ushering in blissful contentment as a happy by-product.

Let's take a vacation home, for instance. In divine will, the acquisition of a second home is an opportunity to deliver joy into the lives of others. You've created a haven where friends and family can get a respite from their daily lives. You may be able to employ a caretaker, bringing perhaps needed income into his life. Maybe you'll Airbnb the house for part of the year, enabling strangers to share in your prosperity and helping to create memorable vacation moments. Living in divine will, these are the thoughts that fill your mind as you dream of your home.

As I wrote up top, I used to steal to get what I wanted. Stuck in self-will, I thought I deserved what I wanted whenever I wanted it. I thought not how my actions might hurt the employees, managers, and coffee shop owners I stole from. At the same time, I felt deeply ashamed and dissatisfied, and my shoplifting habit reinforced a belief that I was a poor child of immigrants who couldn't make money. One day, walking past a West Village townhouse, I realized I couldn't shoplift it. Obvious, I know. But it was an epiphany for me. Theft wasn't a sustainable life strategy. I cried, as I realized stealing wasn't going to give me all the things I really wanted.

After I got sober, my friend launched a weekly mastermind group around money and invited me to join. As I read texts on creating wealth, I realized that making money is actually about generosity and giving. After I started to host retreats and events, I started to notice that when I focused on what I could get—money, acclaim, fame—I felt unfulfilled even when I got what I wanted. When I focused on how I could use my gifts to serve others, and my clients' joy as they transformed, my events got bigger and my income jumped. Funny how that works, huh?

Today, I strive to live in divine will, making amends for all the stealing in my past. I shop a lot at the stores I stole from. I donate to charity. In lines at cafés, I treat complete strangers to coffee and croissants. Try it sometime. It feels so good! The point is, I circulate money. I use it as a tool to bring joy into my life and the lives of others.

Live Above the Law of Self-Will

Assess where you're living in self-will. Are there areas in your life—career or romance, say—where a desire to get is propelled mostly by thoughts about *you*? Under this law, you feel like you can wrangle happiness out of life, but you choke it when you try. Sometimes, people think a surrender to divine will means "giving up," but they're wrong. Surrendering just means allowing the flow of life to work for you by seeing it, and then employing it as your ally.

In meditation, begin to see how realizing your goals will help others, too. As you clarify how your achievements can serve those

◇◇◇◇◇◇◇◇◇◇◇◇◇◇◇◇◇◇◇◇◇◇◇◇◇◇◇◇◇◇◇◇◇

Sometimes, people think a surrender to divine will means "giving up," but they're wrong. Surrendering just means allowing the flow of life to work for you by seeing it, and then employing it as your ally.

◇◇◇◇◇◇◇◇◇◇◇◇◇◇◇◇◇◇◇◇◇◇◇◇◇◇◇◇◇◇◇◇◇

around you, use the tool of asking to request that this divine will paradigm of "get to give" become your modus operandi. Living more and more in this mind-set, you'll want to realize your goals not only to "get" for yourself, but also to bring joy and prosperity into your community. To be clear, it's not an overnight process. Practice these tools daily, observe any perspective shifts, and note the fulfillment and joy you experience.

Verification Point

Look at what you currently have and ask yourself, "How can I use my gifts to create happiness, joy, or opportunities for others?" If you have a winning sense of humor, go make someone laugh. Do it right now! If you're strong, help a friend move. If you're a good listener, call a friend, ask lots of questions, and listen. If you have a great community of friends and colleagues, make valuable introductions and connections.

21

THE LAW OF SEX ENERGY

Sex energy is akin to the Kundalini concept of Shakti, the cosmic energy and creative force that animates the universe and our souls. This instinctual drive to create leads humans to make babies, build the Sistine Chapel, and develop the Internet. The key source of energy that drives our primary and also secondary aims, if we don't channel it in the right way, it leaks into worry, fear, addiction, or promiscuity. On a larger scale, misdirected sex energy leads humans to mine battlefields in Cambodia, build atomic bombs, and drill for oil in Arctic refuges. To avoid misusing sex energy, we can instead leverage it as a tool to awaken, using our intimate relationships as the key lever.

The optimal use of sex energy is to create a masterpiece out of yourself. If you're single and looking, you may think you want to find a partner; what you *really* want is to shape your soul into its highest possibility. If you want a partner who's an artist, cultivate your artistic impulses. If you want a faithful partner, practice faithfulness in all your relationships. In the same way that you use sex energy to create a baby, you can use it to birth yourself anew. Spiritual use of sex energy changes not only *what* you're able to create, but *how* you're able to create it.

In relationships, we tend to misuse sex energy selfishly. Though it's designed to be given generously as a gift, we often look to get high from the sex energy of others. When others lust after us, we feel alive, energized, and confident in a flash. The high tends to be unsustainable, and usually precedes a heavy crash. Couples often seek a replenishing energy from each other that's only available via intimacy with the Divine, and this misuse of sex energy is a kind of vampirism. In trying to suck energy from others, we violate a key spiritual axiom.

Do you remember when I talked about the horizontal and vertical axes of reality? In short, the horizontal is the material and the vertical is the spiritual. When we try to suck energy from others we're sexually attracted to, we're trying to get energy from the horizontal plane. The problem is, there isn't enough energy on this axis to sustain us. Sans an interior spiritual life in relationship with your soul, you thirst for sex energy, and you and your partner try to wrest it from each other, sucking each other dry. Resentment, jealousy, and unhappiness follow. The key to a spiritual life is to learn to *suck sex energy from the vertical line, and exhale it via our actions on the horizontal plane.*

When I first got sober, I used to catch a thrill when flirty guys paid attention to me. I enjoyed it. A lot! At the time, though, my sex energy shot all over the place, and I was only able to manifest noncommittal, confusing relationships with naive, waifish runway models. Empty, meaningless sex. Horizontal line energy. Increasingly dissatisfied, I discussed the issue with my mentor, who showed me key patterns in my sexual relationships. In prayer, I asked for clarity to transform the way I used sexuality.

As I stopped getting high off the advances of random guys, I began to move into an elevated, more dignified state. In fact, as I grew spiritually, it was almost like I became invisible to the flirty crowd. It was kind of like that moment from the original *Star Wars*, where Obi-Wan Kenobi casts a Jedi mind trick to protect his droid friends and tells Darth Vader's storm troopers, "These aren't the droids you're looking for." Though they had aggressively pursued the droids, the troopers repeat, "These aren't the droids we're looking for." As I channeled sex energy into my quest to awaken, I pulled a similar kind of mind trick, making myself invisible to the guys who looked at me like they hadn't eaten in a week and I was a juicy steak.

> As I channeled sex energy into my quest to awaken, I pulled a similar kind of mind trick, making myself invisible to the guys who looked at me like they hadn't eaten in a week and I was a juicy steak.

This spiritual jujitsu also magnetized me to healthy, responsible, emotionally available men. Instead of trying to suck energy from the horizontal line by flashing some skin and getting a hit from some guy turning his head, I focused on drawing energy from the vertical line via asking, meditative, and written spiritual exercises. Six months later, I met the man who's now my husband. Trust me. It works!

Live Above the Law of Sex Energy

Start to dig into this intense energy, realizing that it comes from the vertical, spiritual axis of reality. See how you can draw on this infinite reservoir of spiritual fuel that's available to you in meditation and asking, or prayer. Use these twin practices to plug your soul into divine power, in the same way you plug your phone in to charge at night. Then, when you're all charged up, vent your energies onto the horizontal plane. Deploy them to practice loving-kindness and compassion toward your fellow humans. Use this power to realize the secondary aims you hold for your life on this big, blue planet. Look to cultivate ideal relationships, ones where you both take energy from the spiritual line of reality, and don't try to suck it from each other. Drawing on this endless supply, you'll have limitless amounts of love to give. In a constant flow of giving, you won't expect to receive what he or she can't give, because you're already full and satisfied, munching on the energy of your soul.

Verification Point

Next time you have a crush on someone, start to view him or her as a platonic friend, a sibling, or a kid. For ninety days following a first date, abstain from any kind of sexual contact. During this innocent period, go to museums, movies, and restaurants. Ask yourself questions. Does she make you laugh? Do you actually like his ideas? Do you have a lot to talk about? In this way, you'll cease to objectify this beautiful human in front of you. At the end of this period, not only will you know if you want to make love, you'll make the choice from a new vantage point.

In your journal, make a list of everyone you've ever slept with. When you're done, reflect on how you would have ideally liked to behave in these instances. Then, write about how you'll ideally use your sex energy going forward.

22

THE LAW OF THE SIX PROCESSES OF LOVE

E ver been dumped, then asked yourself, "What the *fuck* just happened?" Me too! Love can be confusing when you don't grasp that it follows six organic processes. These processes can take place over weeks, months, or a lifetime. As a lover, you may cycle through them end to end, or hopscotch over one to land on another. So, whether you're single, hitched, or somewhere in between, as you read below ask yourself, "What process of love am I in?" As you see what stage you're in, confusion will disappear and you'll be able to make choices that empower you as a partner, lover, and friend.

> Ever been dumped, then asked yourself, "What the *fuck* just happened?"

Digestion: Our five senses tend to dominate digestion, the first process. When you're attracted to someone, you "eat" them via sight, sense of smell, and touch. You take in the sounds of their voice. If those senses light up, you later taste a person through kissing and sex. In selecting a partner or even dating someone, it's vital that you want to digest this object of your affection with all five senses. If you disobey your senses—you don't like her smell, you don't like his touch—you may be headed for trouble down the road if you pursue a deeper relationship.

Elimination: Once you've digested, the next process is to eliminate these intense sensations. In elimination, you say "I love you!" over and over. You buy flowers, read him your favorite short stories, or shout her name from a rooftop. If you love someone, it's essential to express it so you can clear space to digest. If you don't eliminate, digestion backs up and you may fall out of love. Of course, after digesting, you may also eject someone from the bubble of love, another way to eliminate.

Perhaps you ignored the warning of your senses and slept with someone you didn't like. In the morning, you wake up, see them asleep next to you, and think, "Ugh, gross." Typically, that's it. It's not going any further. You've moved on. Alternately, if you've been eliminated yourself, you need to understand the person is not choosing to leave you. *The one who's eliminated you can never love you again*. It's a natural process, and there's nothing you can do about it. As painful as it may be, there's no use in pining. Cut the cord on your end as quickly as possible.

The one who's eliminated you can never love you again.

Growth: The next process is growth, which can take place as partners or individually. Growing together, a couple may share new circles of friends, join a shared spiritual community, buy real estate, or build a business. Growing apart, one partner may become an atheist while the other joins a Christian community. One may become a corporate climber, earning the lion's share of household income, while the other is an unemployed writer. Individuals can grow upward, down, or sideways. The downward growth of one partner and the upward growth of the other can lead to a split.

Crime: As a couple grows in a unit, crime enters the picture. Sounds intense, right? A crime can be very small or very big. You may think, "I don't like the way her chin looks. I can't be with someone with that chin." A thought like this can be like a parasite that eats away at intimacy. Other examples of crime: she may emasculate him, flirting with others openly; he may cheat on her. This process tends to be the stage where many relationships falter or break, and if we don't deal with small and big crimes, we never have a chance to heal.

Healing: If a couple splits after crime, the two partners heal apart. When a couple survives crime, both partners need to take responsibility, and open up to new practices outside zones of comfort. Happily, healing can take many forms. Meditate together in the morning. Gaze into your partner's eyes for three to four minutes before making love. Get into tantric sex. See a therapist. Take Kundalini yoga classes, or enroll in a personal development course. Be careful, though. Some of us can get stuck in this phase if we endlessly analyze wounds and orbit the process rather than moving through it.

Regeneration: After you heal, you regenerate. The famous couples therapist Esther Perel says that if you stay married to the same person for fifteen years, you will actually be a partner to three different people. That makes sense! After a successful healing process, you are born anew, and you enter a new state of being, possessing a new consciousness. Ultimately, the birth of a new being body is the aim of our study of the 44 laws, and progress via the six processes is one way to truly reach this state.

Live Above the Law of the
Six Processes of Love

The key takeaway here is to know these six processes exist. So, use what you now know to see what process you're in right now. Digesting a new object of affection? Eliminate loudly and often! Have you been eliminated by someone you loved? Time to grow. Healing from crime? You need to choose whether you want to heal together or apart. If you've been stuck inside a process you can now see clearly, usher in the next one. As you meditate, observe where you've committed crimes, and ask for guidance and strength to overcome them. If a crime weighs on you, share it with someone you trust to keep your confidence—a mentor, spiritual guide, or close friend.

Verification Point

Choose a key relationship—present or past—and examine it through the lens of these six processes. Notice patterns and sticking points. Locate crimes or eliminations you haven't healed. In your journal, describe key moments in the relationship using the framework of the six processes. If the relationship is current, write about the process you're in right now. If it's past, describe the process where it ended. If you can't see patterns clearly, ask for clarity and insight into what to do next in the process you're in. Your aim is to wake up to the organic process that's at play in these stages so you can begin to master the art of relationship.

23

THE LAW OF DESIRE

When I was six years old, I pedaled a bike with training wheels down my block every day, ashamed that I couldn't ride a big-kid, two-wheel bicycle. At night, I dreamt that someone would invent invisibility paint, so I could paint over the training wheels and make them disappear. Adorable as my imaginative six-year-old self was, my dream was a great example of what I call false desire, because my want revolved around being *seen* as someone who could ride a two-wheel bike. But, you see, my true desire was to experience the thrill and freedom of riding a bike without training wheels, and feel the wind in my hair as I raced down a hill.

How do you tune your soul to cultivate such authentic desires? True desire is a multidimensional, textured experience, while false desire tends to present as easy or transactional. A shortcut. False desire is concerned with the image, while true desire is about the soul's bliss. Some spiritual traditions posit that we attain freedom by releasing desires, but I don't subscribe to that belief. On the contrary, I believe that we become who we are

> Some spiritual traditions posit that we attain freedom by releasing desires, but I don't subscribe to that belief. On the contrary, I believe that we become who we are meant to be and achieve our life's purpose by tapping *into* our true desires.

meant to be and achieve our life's purpose by tapping *into* our true desires. Desire is the best tool, not something to be released or shunned. The trick is to distinguish true desire from false.

A telltale sign of a false desire is it appears one-dimensional, rooted in a kind of mechanical motive and method. Let's take a stock kind of goal. You want to become a millionaire. Driven by false desire, you might fantasize about quitting a job or buying a lottery ticket. You may worry you won't ever get there, or you may feel sorry for yourself that you don't have it yet. In such a state, desire leads you around by the nose, and once you've lost control of it, you become its servant. False desire is also myopic, focused only on this narrow outcome, rather than the tangible plans, relationships, and vision you need to create it. You haven't really understood what it means to *desire* one million dollars. In other words, you don't really want it.

> Desire is the best tool, not something to be released or shunned. The trick is to distinguish true desire from false.

A true desire for one million dollars involves the entire experience of realizing a vision in order to give to others. You sincerely want to cultivate genuine human connections with partners, investors, and mentors, and acknowledge the general necessity of doing so. In meditation, perhaps, you discover a challenging, rewarding idea for a business that utilizes your skill set, one you can leverage to turn a healthy profit. You can feel the sensation of the high-thread-count sheet at your fave hotels. You write and revise a vision and make a clear plan. You become an embodiment of your desire.

Live Above the Law of Desire

In order to cultivate authentic desires, we must first touch the soul, as the work of sculpting true desire is internal, not external. Desire to change inwardly is the real work. When our interior life shifts, our external world transforms, in the same way the frog turned into a prince in the classic fairy tale. In your meditation, visualize your desires, and practice asking for them to be revealed to you. Ask yourself tough questions like, "What do I *really* want?" Begin to separate out the desires rooted in what others think of you, and those based in experiences and feelings you actually want to have.

Use the tools of asking and meditation to discern true versus false desire. One way to determine the quality of a desire is to sit and listen. The true desire will usually manifest as a soft, gentle voice, while false ones will provoke anxiety and arrive with loud intensity. Paradoxically, a key aspect of an authentic desire is that you may feel ashamed of wanting it. Typically, these are desires we may fear we won't ever realize. Pay attention to this sense, especially, as it can be a key indicator you're on the right track. When you're honest with yourself about what you truly want, the steps you need to take to achieve what you want tend to reveal themselves. Use these guidelines, along with your morning practice, to sort out true and false desires.

Verification Point

In your journal, write out one of your desires in the present tense, as if you already possess it. Start with "I now have . . ." and inscribe details into your vision. When I first practiced this exercise, I wrote very specifically. I wrote about the kinds of close friends I desired—their attitudes, lifestyles, and vocations. I specified furniture styles for the home I wanted, countries I'd visit, and museums where I'd lead meditations. Be bold. Think expansively. It's okay to want it all! If you'd like, you can read your desire to a trusted friend.

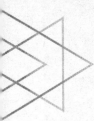

24

THE LAW OF PAYMENT

The Law of Payment poses a key question: do you want to pay on the front end or the back end? On the front end, payment requires an initial layout of time, energy, and effort. On the back end, payment looks like a shortcut initially, only to drain us of time, energy, and effort over the long term, sometimes for our entire lives. Clearly, I'm not just talking about money here. Payment is required for every exchange, whether spiritual, financial, or relational, and that payment can be either constructive or destructive. In other words, the *way* you pay can build you up, or it can tear you down. In fact, money is the lowest form of payment. The highest is your presence: the gift of *you*, your essence.

> ◇◇◇◇◇◇◇◇◇◇◇◇◇◇◇◇◇◇◇◇◇◇
>
> In fact, money is the lowest form of payment. The highest is your presence: the gift of *you*, your essence.
>
> ◇◇◇◇◇◇◇◇◇◇◇◇◇◇◇◇◇◇◇◇◇◇

Payment on the front end is key to a fulfilling, satisfied life. Exhaust yourself in workouts for six months. Get six-pack abs.

◇◇◇◇◇◇◇◇◇◇◇◇◇◇◇◇◇◇◇◇◇◇◇◇◇◇

Payment on the front end is key to a fulfilling, satisfied life.

◇◇◇◇◇◇◇◇◇◇◇◇◇◇◇◇◇◇◇◇◇◇◇◇◇◇

Invest time, money, and energy to climb K2. Experience transcendence at the summit. Work the uncomfortable practice of daily meditation and asking. Reap the rewards of clarity, joy, and a sense of purpose. Do the mundane work of being attentive to your finances, and track income and expenses. Experience long-term security, prosperity, and a sense of wealth. Practice the restraint and discipline of eating foods that fill you with energy. Gain the benefits of fitness and health.

Payment on the back end leads to an erratic, boom-bust life filled with pain and unhappiness. Eat a candy bar or a pint of ice cream. Shoot yourself up with a quick sugar high, short-term bliss, and a moment of fleeting joy. Pay on the back end with fatigue, zits, and stomach pain. Drink a bottle of wine or snort a line of cocaine to get into a higher state for a moment. Pay on the back end with a hangover, grogginess, and guilt. Get into a drunken one-night stand and feel high for an hour. Pay later with an unsatisfying sex life, regret, and shame.

I recently contracted with a boutique luxury hotel on the Amalfi Coast to lead a meditation workshop on site. Since there are no direct flights from New York to Naples, the trip was around eighteen hours door-to-door. Long layover. Connecting flight. Fitful sleep. Airplane head cold. Two-hour drive from the airport to hotel. To be clear, I'm not complaining! Positano is gorgeous and the coast is to die for. But as we drove the winding roads hugging the Mediterranean, my husband wondered if all the travel was really worth it: "Why not just stay home?" he asked.

Hours later, as we sipped shaken espresso nearly naked on a balcony overlooking the Mediterranean, he changed his tune. The Amalfi Coast is a truly magical place, and over the course of the next week we had incredible experiences. We had paid, and were now reaping the benefits of what we had paid for. While travel to exotic locales can seem glamorous, even when it's free, we need to be willing to pay in energy, sickness, time, and exhaustion. The payment process tends to be uncomfortable, and it's the experience of paying that we tend to try and avoid. Often, we look for the payoff without relishing the payment, and this is when we tend to create problems.

Honesty is a powerful form of up-front payment. Let's say you're a woman in the market for a relationship. After a few months of dating a guy, and things seem like they're about to turn serious, he backpedals and says he's not looking for a committed relationship. He'd rather keep things easy-breezy, no strings attached, noncommittal. Want to pay on the front end? Tell him what you want. Lay it on the line, say you want a committed relationship, and take a plunge of courage. If you choose this path, you will have paid. If he fails to agree, move on. I promise you that by paying up front now with honesty, you'll take one step closer to the relationship you desire, even if it's with someone else.

The alternative is to pay on the back end. Lay out some mealy half-agreement with what he's saying. Lie to yourself and him on the front end, grasp a few more months of emotional satisfaction from your relationship, and hope for the thing you want in the future. But you still haven't paid. The payment will arrive when the gap between what you really want and the terms he already stated up front clash. Then you'll pay on the back end with grief, tears, and dissatisfaction.

I used to try to avoid payment my whole life, and that behavior ended up costing so much more over the long term. In my twenties, I used to get compliments all the time on how thin I was. I loved it. People used to ask me, "What's your secret?" Ha! My secret was a heroin habit masquerading as a fitness plan. The

◇◇◇◇◇◇◇◇◇◇◇◇◇◇◇◇◇◇◇◇◇◇◇◇◇◇◇

I used to get compliments all the time on how thin I was. I loved it. People used to ask me, "What's your secret?" Ha! My secret was a heroin habit masquerading as a fitness plan.

◇◇◇◇◇◇◇◇◇◇◇◇◇◇◇◇◇◇◇◇◇◇◇◇◇◇◇

back-end payment was that I was literally killing myself. Today, I live as happy and fit as ever, but I pay for it up front. I use all kinds of tools. Breathwork. Intuitive eating. Minimal flour and sugar. Yoga. Gym. I get the same look, and I don't have to die like a rock star. Trust me. It's the way to live.

Live Above the Law of Payment

Start to pay up front in all areas of your life. You need to put forth effort and attention on the front end, or you'll be paying on the back end. Awareness of this law strips away the naïveté that makes us think we can get stuff for "free." Of course, we do manifest magic, but the spiritual work that readies us to receive miracles is the *way* we pay for them. In order to be a vessel that the universe pours its energy through, you need to pay to refine your vessel via meditation and asking, and a healthy diet and exercise. Yes, the highest form of payment is the gift of *you*, your essence.

Above this law, you always feel worthy because you know exactly how you got to where you are. You will begin to embody the saying, "I make my own luck." People often ask me why I no longer do drugs or drink, especially when they can sometimes lead to the most blissful altered states you can imagine. I always tell them the same thing. I live in those states all the time today, and I know exactly how to get back when I'm kicked out. A heightened state of life is available to you, and when you pay on the front end you will not only know how to get to this state easily, you'll be able to lead others there as well.

Verification Point

Ask yourself, "Where in my life am I not paying on the front end, while expecting great rewards on the back end?" Once you've identified something you want that you haven't paid for, look for ways you can start to pay on the front end. Be honest to pay for what you really want. Go to the gym to pay for six-pack abs. Meditate to pay for freedom. Observe how your life unfolds once you're willing to put in the time, energy, and effort required to pay up front.

Ask yourself, "Where in my life am I not paying on the front end, while expecting great rewards on the back end?"

25

THE LAW OF KNOWLEDGE, BEING, AND UNDERSTANDING

I was never great at math, but here's a kind of metaphysical equation: knowledge + being = understanding. This mystical sequence is the holy trinity of experience. But it also presents a key dilemma: if we acquire knowledge, and we're not in a conscious being state, we can't *understand* it. On Instagram, you might scroll past a wise Einstein quote the same way you scroll past a McDonald's ad. No judgment. We all do it! But in a conscious state, you can tune your being to frequencies that elevate you, and tune out the ones that don't.

I was never great at math, but here's a kind of metaphysical equation: knowledge + being = understanding.

Since your state of being is like a muscle, in order to live above this law, you'll need to work it out to make it stronger.

Think about it this way. In a yoga class, the teacher may explain precisely how to do a pose. She may even demonstrate the perfect technique. Now you have the knowledge of how to do it. But you may not be able to actually do it, so you don't *understand* the pose yet. In order to understand it, you have to apply your being state to the pose by practicing it. This may take quite some time depending on your level of proficiency and the complexity of the pose. Eventually, after you apply your being to the pose through repeated practice, you are able to complete it perfectly. Now you understand it.

As you cultivate conscious states of being over a lifetime, you can transform your level of understanding. This is why believers read landmark spiritual texts like the Bible or the Torah many times over the course of their lives: so they can ascertain new levels of understanding. The text doesn't change. The reader does. This is also true of literary works, and applies to this book, as well. Designed as a manual for living life awake, you will be best served by returning to it time and again to glean new insights and grasp new concepts.

Okay, great. So how do you shift your state of being to grasp the understanding available in knowledge you take in? Before you watch a film, view a work of art, or read a text, ask the universe to reveal its deeper truth to you. Spend a minute in silence, breathe through your nose, and ask to be shifted to a state of love to receive the most spiritual beauty possible. In conversation with friends or at work, listen carefully, and pause before you respond. These practices will help you filter out noise and cut straight to the essence of knowledge presented to you.

Recently, I had a client who suffered from alcoholism. The illness ran in his family, and he knew beyond a shadow of a doubt he had this problem. In other words, he had the knowledge. He desperately wanted to get sober, but couldn't seem to piece together more than a week or so of sobriety at a time. In our work together, I suggested that he immerse himself in the practices of twelve-step programs. He read the literature, learned some concepts, and moved on with his life. To put it another way, he got more knowledge! Guess what? He relapsed again.

As we reviewed this law again and again, I convinced him that to understand sobriety—in this case, to actually *get* sober—he was going to have to apply his being to the books he read and the words he heard at meetings. In other words, he was going to have to do some work. He finally started to pray, meditate, go to meetings, and get a sponsor. Once he did, he started to stay sober. He finally understood sobriety, and hasn't taken a drink since.

Live Above the Law of Knowledge, Being, and Understanding

In *The Power of Myth*, Joseph Campbell writes, "I don't believe people are looking for the meaning of life as much as they are looking for the experience of being alive." I love this quote; it's so powerful! The way I read it, though, he implies that experience, or being, is superior to meaning, or knowledge. But the ability to make meaning distinguishes humans. An eagle experiences the wonder of flying, for example, yet doesn't have the capacity to reflect on its elegance or power. Humans do, though. So why sell ourselves short by elevating one or the other?

> The use of meditative stillness, in concert with a big, bold life lived out loud, mixes the best of both worlds.

To me, these qualities are equally important, and equally available. It's when we mix meaning and experience—or knowledge and being—that we *understand* our lives on a visceral level. The use of meditative stillness, in concert with a big, bold life lived out loud, mixes the best of both worlds. In this state, we can live peak experiences, and observe ourselves as we do so. This quality is key to a meditative lifestyle, and creates the kind of perspective we can really use as we pursue happiness.

Verification Point

For this verification, get into a heightened state to take in knowledge. First, select a spiritual text. It could be a passage or book of the Bible, a poem by Rumi or Kahlil Gibran, or an excerpt from the Bhagavad Gita or Torah. Ideally, it's a text you have some familiarity with. Before you begin, spend a minute in silence, split your attentions, and ask to have the text's deeper truth revealed to you. As you read, practice *being* with the text, and notice the mysteries it reveals as new understandings unfold.

26

THE LAW OF CONSCIOUS
SUFFERING

Suffering is bad, right? Well, yeah, sometimes. But it's complicated. As Jean-Pierre de Caussade, an eighteenth-century priest, wrote, "God instructs the heart, not by ideas, but by pains and contradictions." Suffering can instruct the heart, and when it does, its value is limitless. But the process also takes three distinct forms—unnecessary, necessary, and conscious—that shape our lives in profoundly different ways. In treating suffering, it's vital to suss out the kind that confronts you, so you can either get rid of it, use it to heal and elevate, or intentionally create it to wake up!

Unnecessary suffering is really the worst. Jealousy. Resentment. Shame. Worry. Insecurity. Self-doubt. These emotional states can be almost addictive, a go-to method of handling frustration, disappointment, or unrealized expectations. But we don't actually heal or grow via unnecessary suffering, as it keeps us asleep to infinite possibility. This type appears to happen *to* us automatically, and we may feel like it exerts control over us. The good news is that it's *unnecessary*, so the goal is simply to eliminate it, or at least turn its volume down so low you can barely hear it.

Necessary suffering is a tragic life event, the kind that visits nearly all. Breast cancer. A violent car crash. The unexpected, sudden death of a loved one. This form of suffering is powerful, and it's designed to catapult you to a new level of consciousness. I lived through this when I cradled my daughter, Ula, dead in my arms. Her death cracked open my heart, allowing me to fully experience painful emotions that led me to my soul. When you transpose emotional trauma into a spiritual experience, you're using the emotional center to wake up. Today, pain and pleasure present to me as two sides of a coin; any deeply felt experience that shocks me into a state of presence is a valuable gift.

> Her death cracked open my heart, allowing me to fully experience painful emotions that led me to my soul.

Conscious suffering is the type you choose to create to wake up. Its practices embody suffering in the sense that they require sacrifice, pain, and levels of discomfort. They're conscious because they're *chosen*. Meditate thirty minutes every day. Cut sugar and flour from your diet. Donate to a worthy cause, enough that it stings. Risk death to climb Everest. Puke up and shit your shorts to run a marathon. Suffer! Of course, the opportunity to suffer consciously is a profound privilege, one we fritter away with worry, fear, or indecision—the suffering that has zero value. The logic of this type

> Suffering is coming one way or another, so why not choose the form it's going to take on your own fucking terms?

goes like this: suffering is coming one way or another, so why not choose the form it's going to take on your own fucking terms?

When I was twenty-four, I woke up in bed six nights in a row to an ethereal voice. It said, simply, "You are dying." Every night, for six nights! No drugs, no hallucination, just a voice. On the sixth night, I finally asked, "Okay, if that's true, what can I do?" The voice replied, "Don't eat." Terrified and a little crazed, I obeyed, and lost thirteen pounds in three weeks. One night, I looked down at my belly and saw a large bulge. I walked into the living room and showed it to my dad. He took one look at me and said, "You are either three months pregnant or you have a very big tumor." I wasn't pregnant.

He picked up the phone and called his former client and family friend—a practicing OB/GYN—who admitted me to a hospital in Great Neck, Long Island, hours later. It turned out I had a super-dense seven-pound tumor in my uterus, roughly the size of a large grapefruit, and my doctor explained that I needed surgery the next morning. He told me that there was about a five percent chance he could save my uterus. More likely, I'd never be able to have children.

But the four-hour surgery was successful, and he was able to remove all traces of the tumor. He explained, though, that if I didn't birth a child in the next two years, the tumor would return and I'd never be able to have children. I thought, "Well, I'm not about to have kids anytime soon, so I guess that's that." I couldn't have known how wrong I was.

Fast forward two years, to the night God took my daughter, Ula, back home. I don't know if you know this, but when an infant dies suddenly, detectives question the parents first. After they interviewed me I fell to the floor, stricken with grief in that small hospital room. Utterly destroyed, I also felt the faintest hint of hope. Ula had cured my uterus, and given me a new life. Sprawled on the floor, face wet with tears, I clasped my hands and said, "God, please help me. I don't know how to pray." That same voice spoke back, "That's right. You don't."

In that moment, I grasped the lived quality of necessary suffering, though I didn't know the term at the time. The loss of Ula healed my uterus and woke me up enough to ask in prayer. Though it took two more years to kick heroin, in retrospect this moment was the beginning of the end of my old life, and the birth of a new one. Necessary suffering can wake us up to limitless power, if we let it work its magic.

Live Above the Law of Conscious Suffering

To live above this law, the aim is threefold: eliminate the unnecessary, embrace the necessary, and create the conscious. In other words, misery is optional and pain is guaranteed, so why not create conscious pain to wake yourself up? Become aware of worry, fear, or shame—whatever unnecessary sufferings frustrate you. Notice moments where they kick up and ask, "Do I want to be rid of this?" When tragedy occurs, as it will, embrace it via tools like grief counseling, and ask to see how you can leverage emotional pain as a spiritual asset. Use meditation to create a deep reservoir of interior calm.

Choose to trade unnecessary suffering for conscious choice. Though you may think unnecessary suffering happens to you, you actually create it. So, why not replace it with conscious, constructive pain? It has real value, and yields tangible rewards! I know, I know. It's hard. But the more you suffer consciously as part of a daily routine, the less emotional garbage you'll have to handle on a daily basis. To be clear, I don't mean you ought to invite necessary suffering into your life to grow spiritually. But you can invite conscious pain into your life by choice in order to awaken. Trust me. I do it every day!

Verification Point

In order to verify this law, select a form of conscious suffering you feel called to: physical exercise, volunteer service, or any other practice that pushes you beyond your comfort zone. Begin to practice it. If thirty minutes a day of meditation is still a challenge, stick to that. Notice that you won't have the needed energy to practice conscious suffering until you become willing to let go of its unnecessary cousin.

◇◇◇◇◇◇◇◇◇◇◇◇◇◇◇◇◇◇◇◇◇◇◇◇◇◇◇◇

You won't have the needed energy to practice conscious suffering until you become willing to let go of its unnecessary cousin.

◇◇◇◇◇◇◇◇◇◇◇◇◇◇◇◇◇◇◇◇◇◇◇◇◇◇◇◇

27

THE LAW OF HUMAN TYPES

*C*an I tell you a secret? A system of ancient spiritual wisdom exists, one you can use as a kind of toolkit to make your life *so* much easier. For some reason, though, it's kept under wraps, and only pops up in pricey workshops. Sourced from the same metaphysics as Ayurvedic philosophy, the system posits seven human types: Lunar, Venusian, Mercurial, Saturn, Martial, Jovial, and Solar. Since most of us live out of sync with our type, once we discover it, the results can be revolutionary. We can design lives that play to our strengths, minimize weaknesses, and align to our true purpose. A quick word before we get started, though. This system could easily fill a book on its own, so by necessity the words below present only a broad overview.

> We can design lives that play to our strengths, minimize weaknesses, and align to our true purpose.

The Lunar: This type presents as thin and frail-looking. Often pale, lanky, and with bad vision, Lunars typically sport glasses. Willful and with a love of the word "no," this type tends to possess incredible focus, even obsessiveness, and a meticulous attentiveness to detail. Attracted at times to a darker side of life, they may disappear for stretches of time, only to reappear in the lives of friends and colleagues as if nothing had happened. They tend to orbit shiny things, from solar types to innovative, high-tech tools. Think Steve Jobs, Spike Lee, or Gandhi. As leaders, they possess tremendous vision, but can be incredibly difficult to work with, as their obsessive, singular focus can be both a curse and a blessing.

The Venusian: Venusians like to lie around a lot à la Venus, the goddess of love. Full heads of hair, puffy lips, curvy. Joyful and funny, relaxed and easygoing, the Venusian indulges pleasure in all its forms. Lots of leisure in the life of the Venusian. Sex, chocolate, ganja, and great meals. Think Renaissance painting subjects. Some Venusians in pop culture are Winnie the Pooh, Elizabeth Taylor, and Elvis Presley. In its lower state, problems with this type can include laziness, carelessness, and passivity.

The Mercurial: This type tends to have high levels of mental energy, which they use to persuade, convince, or manipulate. Feisty, vain, people-loving. Glittery eyes. Muscular, lean, and tiny, this type is tightly wound, like a ball of energy. Sensitive but resilient, a Mercurial can withstand many difficulties. Fast-talking and perceptive, they generate thoughts and words at a brisk clip. Great salesmen. Masters of messaging. Johnny Depp. Penélope Cruz. David Blaine. Given the right circumstances, though, this type also makes for the perfect criminal personality. Cheerful and witty, with a sunny persona, they can also be argumentative, sarcastic, and cynical.

The Saturn: A big-picture thinker, the Saturn type is a natural leader. Dominant. Tall. Intimidating. Highly analytical, the

Saturn sees the way parts connect to the whole, and makes an effective politician, diplomat, or other leader. Abraham Lincoln. Barack Obama. Sigourney Weaver. They tend to subtly lead with their presence alone, and those around them intuitively look to them as authority figures. In dark moments, they can be fierce and cruel. The Saturn type hates to follow others, and struggles when others lead or challenge their dominance.

The Martial: This type is named after Mars, the god of war, and for good reason. Warriorlike, this type loves rules, order, and justice. Quite passionate, they are quick to anger, often defensive, and can be rude and overly direct. Often short- and hot-tempered, the Martial lives to be right. Believing strongly in doing as they're told and obeying rules, they're bothered by those that break them. Self-righteous and loyal, they tend to speak in commands and judge the world around them. Martin Luther King. Hillary Clinton. Lena Dunham. With a strong sense of right and wrong, they care deeply about the world being a good place, and they want to be the ones to fix it.

The Jovial: Jovials have large, boisterous personalities and tend to present as stout and fleshy. Rosy cheeks, big laughs, and top-heavy bodies characterize this type. Big. Cheerful. Fun. Larger than life. Oprah. Guy Fieri. Santa Claus. While they are maternal, compassionate, and generous, they can often overindulge, especially with food, and are therefore typically heavyset. They thrive as caretakers tasked with overseeing others, and make great hosts, chefs and hoteliers, as they enjoy cooking for and entertaining others.

The Solar: This type presents as naive and optimistic, wide-eyed, and beautiful. Super sexy, sensual, and charismatic, everyone tends to be attracted to him or her. Quite vain, this type loves to be fawned over as the center of attention. Solars tend to be actors, singers, and performers. Innocent, sensitive, idealistic dreamers. Ethereal and childlike. Think Michael Jackson, Winona Ryder, or Kurt Cobain. Burning so brightly, Solars tend to be not long for this world, often flaming out at a young age. I know because I am one, and I was on a typically solar self-destructive path until I discovered tools to sustain the bright fire inside me. So don't worry. You don't need to die young to be this type!

Live Above the Law of Human Types

To live above this law, look to leverage what works in a given body type, while also striving to push past its weaknesses.

- The Lunar may practice being cooperative, and resist the urge to disappear for long stretches of time.

- A Venusian ought to look to balance leisure with athleticism and exercise.

- A Mercurial can practice being a better listener to set himself free from self-absorption.

- A Saturn type ought to choose to soften up a bit, freeing herself from taking her own dominance so seriously.

- At times, the Martial can look to see how he can be more even-tempered and agreeable.

- A Jovial can look to check his motives when he's being giving, ensuring his aim is to serve others, rather than mechanically fix everything.

- A Solar ought to harness her charismatic, attractive energy to strengthen the dignity and grace of the soul.

By taking actions that oppose the natural inclinations of a body type, you'll ensure that you don't just "fall asleep" under a given set of character traits and live life on autopilot. At the same time, realize that your greatest assets lie in your type's traits, so embrace and harness them to your advantage.

By taking actions that oppose the natural inclinations of a body type, you'll ensure that you don't just "fall asleep" under a given set of character traits and live life on autopilot.

Verification Point

Which type are you? As you observe your tendencies, you'll discover your type over time. In order to verify it, though, observe your ways of being in the world, and ask yourself questions like the ones below.

- If you're somewhat frail, meticulous, and detail-oriented, and like to spend time alone, perhaps you're the Lunar type.

- If you're a bit overweight, super-easygoing, a friend to all, and relish life's pleasures, you're likely Venusian.

- Are you a somewhat sneaky, mischievous fast-talker? Perhaps you're Mercurial.

- If you're dominant, tall, masculine, and love to be in charge, you're likely Saturn.

- Do you love to organize others and need to be "right" all the time, knowing that you're hot-tempered? Sounds like you're a Martial.

- If you're fun-loving and jolly, love to take care of others, and possess maternal tendencies, you may be Jovial.

- Are you sensual, somewhat naive, and enthusiastic? You may be Solar.

28

THE LAW OF CHIEF FEATURES

Superman beats the bad guys because he knows his Achilles' heel: kryptonite. Sure, he can fly, too. But if he didn't know kryptonite kills him, some supervillain would take him down. Unlike the Man of Steel, though, most of us live unaware of our key weaknesses, or chief features. Under this law, our chief features—a weakness that takes you down—present as one, or several, of nine types. Dominance. Laziness. Power. Willfulness. Invisibility. Vanity. Naïveté. Lunacy. Fear. For example, I tend to feature vanity and naïveté, functions of my Solar personality. When you're aware of a weakness that drains your powers, you take a first step to being a superhero in your own life.

Dominance: Under the feature of dominance, you need to be totally in charge at all times. This weakness—often found in the Saturn type—tells you it's not quite good enough to be one of several powerful persons in a room. You need to be at the top. Unaware of your need to lead pretty much always, you may wonder why you feel so resentful or angry when following another's lead or fulfilling another's wishes at work. But when you know that your chief feature is dominance, you can grasp why you're troubled in those moments, and choose to pause and ask for calm. At the same time, you *need* to lead. So do it. Go lead.

Laziness: Under the feature of laziness, you play passive, thinking your efforts don't really make a difference in the world. Unaware of this key weakness typically associated with the Venusian type, you may feel helpless and think, "I don't really have what it takes," as you watch the world go by. In some ways, though, this trait flows from a deep sense that, really, all is at it should be. So, if you feature laziness, you can actually turn it into an asset. Relish your unique privilege to combine your easygoing nature with optimism, and act. Relaxed humans who act to effect change are a rare breed indeed. So go be one.

Power: The power feature—common to Mercurial and Martial types—drives you to one-up others, incessantly comparing yourself to peers or colleagues at every turn. Seeking power, you look for lots of status and praise, especially in a peer group or industry. Easily jealous, it may pain you deeply when a rival garners an accolade in your presence. Insecure, you want above all to be *seen* as powerful and important. In order to transmute this feature, find ways to celebrate and applaud your peers. See how you can collaborate and support, rather than destroy or tear down.

Willfulness: With the feature of willfulness, you try to assert yourself by being disagreeable and stubborn. Often affecting the Lunar type, this weakness puts you in love with your power to simply say "no." Usually, though, willful ones eventually end up doing what others ask anyway. To live above this feature, notice when you're about to disagree simply for the pleasure and power it gives you. Then, choose to skip the "no" and just go straight to a "yes." Ask, or pray, to be cooperative and generous with others. Strive to collaborate and reach consensus. You'll save yourself so much time, energy, and effort when you do.

Invisibility: Invisibility is akin to a kind of nonexistence, or an effort to disappear. Common to the Lunar, this weakness leads you to whisper your words and shrink away from colleagues, friends, and family. Often hidden by dark clothes or glasses, you may feel unseen or unheard. But is it really a surprise, since you hide yourself so often? To live above here, trade contacts for glasses and wear bright colors. Think Clark Kent and Superman. Speak up, assert yourself, and become visible to the world. It waits for you.

Vanity: Vanity is my personal favorite, and applies mostly to the Solar type. In vanity, you like to look at yourself in the mirror, love to see pictures of yourself, and long to be photographed. Nothing wrong with that! Caring too deeply about what others think, though, you may worry often how others perceive you, and obsessively try to decode their thoughts. At its extreme, vanity can become self-absorption, so be mindful of its darker tendencies. At the same time, relish being the center of attention, and indulge your desire to be visible. Famous, even! With a visible platform in society you can facilitate many charitable efforts.

Naïveté: Unmindful of mundane details of reality, naïveté leads you to pay lots of attention to possibility and potential. On the plus side, this feature—often found in Solar and Jovial types—can lead you to take entrepreneurial risks, since you don't pay attention to all the reasons a venture might fail. Unaware of this trait, though, you may jump into relationships doomed from the outset, or launch a business without research to assess its viability. So get grounded. Pay attention to warning signs, and use foresight to make good decisions. You can be a dreamer with your head in the clouds, but keep your feet firmly planted on the planet.

Lunacy: It sounds extreme, but hot-tempered and emotional, you lash out with little warning under this feature. Speeding from zero to ten on the emotional Richter scale in an instant, you display a high degree of volatility. Common to the Lunar, this weakness can be overcome by a steady effort to respond, rather than react. So, use divided attention to observe yourself as your temper flares. Breathe and pause to restrain yourself, and in addition to meditation, channel a hot temper into exercise or creative projects.

Fear: A feature common to us all. Fear keeps us out of the present moment and in constant thought about future worst-case scenarios or worry about the consequences of the past. In the present moment, fear doesn't exist. There's a reason they call it "the present," since it really is the ultimate gift of all, this blissed-out state of neutrality. So to find freedom from fear, observe when it comes. Divide your attention to float above it, and ask for relief and trust. When you see that fear does nothing but clog the mind and body with unnecessary tension, stress, and thoughts, it's easier to shed, and live above.

Live Above the Law of Chief Features

Throughout your day, note which features pop up most often at home, at work, and in private. See the weaknesses that drain your energy. Awareness alone can work wonders, as it's the first step to freeing yourself from a feature's darker tendencies. Now that you can see reality more clearly, observe the moments when your chief feature activates, and capitalize on these moments to dissolve its destructive qualities and accent its empowering aspects. You can only start

◇◇◇◇◇◇◇◇◇◇◇◇◇◇◇◇◇◇◇◇◇◇◇◇◇◇

You can only start to optimize potential—realize your superpowers, if you will—when you clarify a great weakness.

◇◇◇◇◇◇◇◇◇◇◇◇◇◇◇◇◇◇◇◇◇◇◇◇◇◇

to optimize potential—realize your superpowers, if you will—when you clarify a great weakness. Once you identify your chief feature, you'll never be blindsided by it again.

◇◇◇◇◇◇◇◇◇◇◇◇◇◇◇◇◇◇◇◇◇

Once you identify your chief feature, you'll never be blindsided by it again.

◇◇◇◇◇◇◇◇◇◇◇◇◇◇◇◇◇◇◇◇◇

Verification Point

Once you recognize a chief feature, own it out loud. Look into the mirror and say, "I like to disappear," or "I am vain as fuck!" Be grateful for the new awareness. Someone might say to you, "God, you're so willful," and you'll be able to say, "Tell me something I don't know!" Now that you can see into your blind spot, use this new line of sight to activate a fresh worldview.

29

THE LAW OF ACCUMULATORS

I know it's not easy to hear, but your soul is starving. Even in a life filled with rich experiences—world travel, falling in love, creative peaks—the soul rarely gets a chance to absorb and digest our vital moments. Why? Well, the body and mind—the first accumulator—always eat first. You see, the body and mind are like ravenous, unrefined little beasties that munch away on your experiences, digesting them before the soul—the second accumulator—even gets a taste. The trick is, the body and mind will always process experiences first. In order to hit the second accumulator, we need to practice patience, and pass through the first phase to feed the soul.

> ◇◇◇◇◇◇◇◇◇◇◇◇◇◇◇◇◇◇◇◇◇◇◇
> I know it's not easy to hear, but your soul is starving.
> ◇◇◇◇◇◇◇◇◇◇◇◇◇◇◇◇◇◇◇◇◇◇◇

Okay, let's start with a typical perfect moment: sunset, beach, summer. The sun feels so good on your skin, and your tan looks amaze. The body loves it. Then, the mind thinks, "Oh, wow, I've gotta get this on Instagram." So you put it up. Then, the mind wonders, "How many likes did I get?"

So, you check your phone. So many likes! The mind's like, "I did a great job on this beach today." You lie back, and soak in the last sunrays. The problem is, *you* haven't absorbed this experience. Your body and mind fed, but your soul's still hungry. No judgment. I love Instagram! But the first accumulator is a thief.

If you push past the Instagram moment to stay in the now, you may start to sense discomfort. The mind might shriek, "I already got my experience!" But if you stay in stillness and silence to observe the sunset, the soul pokes its head out to digest. *Our eyes are like a spiritual mouth, and the soul feeds on beauty*: the bliss of the blue sea, the wonder of the pink sky, gratitude for the heat and light, and how precious it is to be anything at all on a planet spinning through space. This moment where the soul feeds is a space of real bliss. But it's typically a process we resist in all areas of our lives.

Resistance arrives after the first accumulator has fed to its fill, and shows up in all areas of our lives. It's the point in meditation, usually ten to fifteen minutes in, when you think, "I really have more important things to do right now." It's the moment in a hot yoga class when you want to give up, or the point where you evade soulful eye contact in bed because you want to get to orgasm. Ultimately, it's the moment you run away from your self. You've forgotten what brings you bliss, so you resist it. You're looking in all the wrong places. It's right here.

Several years ago, I sat in front of a Rembrandt self-portrait at the Metropolitan Museum of Art. As I gazed, a thought struck.

"You're hungry, Biet. You should go out and get a snack!" As I stood, though, I realized if I ate that snack, I'd starve my soul. So I sat back down. I was going to have to drag myself through discomfort if I wanted to feed my soul with beauty. Soon, I reaped the rewards. As I sat and gazed at the art, the colors deepened, and for a moment the painting leapt out at me in three dimensions, almost like an extremely pleasurable, natural hallucination. I had allowed the great master's art to touch my soul. I felt so replenished and alive!

Live Above the Law of Accumulators

Start by making small, powerful moves. Present your meals on a beautifully set table from time to time. Chew food slowly and silently, and experience the taste and pleasure of the meal. In your sex life, make lots of eye contact, light candles, play soft music, and use lots of foreplay, kissing softly and deeply. In moments of pause in a conversation, practice silence even though it feels awkward. Watch as energy rushes in and you feel suddenly super-present to your senses.

Get willing to sit through discomfort to reach the soul. Choose to up the time you spend under level C influences, such as paintings, classical music, spiritual texts. Realize you elevate consciousness as you do. Listen to a jazz record or symphony not as background music, but as the main event. Take every opportunity to be present to the moment.

Harness the energy you accumulate to access limitless, godlike energy. Want to climb Denali? Have a burning desire to build a business? Access to this energy can deliver capacity to realize our greatest ambitions and dreamiest projects. Of course, for some, it's possible to accomplish these goals on the first accumulator alone, but the baggage that comes along with this method tends to be burnout, stress, and exhaustion.

Verification Point

Find a big, beautiful sunset, and meditate in front of it with open eyes. Observe yourself as you pass through discomfort when you begin to fill your soul, and note the deeper level of experience you achieve in this state of presence. Resist the call to pull your phone out. Note the level of discomfort that arises, as well as the deep pleasure you eventually reach by engaging with the sunset via your intentional extra effort.

◇◇◇◇◇◇◇◇◇◇◇◇◇◇◇◇◇◇◇◇◇◇◇◇◇◇◇◇◇◇◇

Find a big, beautiful sunset, and meditate in front of it with open eyes.

◇◇◇◇◇◇◇◇◇◇◇◇◇◇◇◇◇◇◇◇◇◇◇◇◇◇◇◇◇◇◇

30

THE LAW OF UNNECESSARY TALK

Ever watched a vintage organ grinder monkey clash its small cymbals? From a conscious point of view, that's what unnecessary talk is: little more than automatic noise. Like the monkey controlled by a puppeteer, when we talk, we just pass along messages programmed into us in school, at work, or at home. Gossip. Small talk. Cynicism. When we *speak*, though, we communicate via the soul in a state of alert presence. Unnecessary talk wastes energy; speaking creates energy. To live above this law, we must learn to practice speaking, and gin up energy with our language and words.

〈〈〈〈〈〈〈〈〈〈〈〈〈〈〈〈〈〈〈〈〈〈〈〈〈〈〈〈〈
Unnecessary talk wastes energy;
speaking creates energy.
〈〈〈〈〈〈〈〈〈〈〈〈〈〈〈〈〈〈〈〈〈〈〈〈〈〈〈〈〈

Practicing the art of speaking is like tuning to a radio frequency few people can hear. This art requires presence and effort, and enables us to direct conscious ideas and inspiration into the world. To speak consciously, divide your attention three times to observe your words, audience, and inner state. This way, you can almost slow down time, choose words carefully, and edit sentences as you speak. As you split your attention, you can cultivate an inner state of silence, even as you speak.

In fact, our ability to speak rather than talk depends on our ability to practice silence. So often in our lives, we destroy the value of high-energy experiences by chatting about them casually afterward, leaking energy we could have retained. When we meditate, climb a mountain, sit through a spiritual service, read a conscious book, or view a conscious film, we get energy to harness, giving us spiritual power. Unfortunately, after receiving this incredible gift, we leak power by chatting about an experience mindlessly.

> Talk is cheap; speaking is priceless.

In silence, though, you can stop leaking. With a meditative practice, you can actually seal energy inside yourself, and use it to illuminate your soul to others. You can also use it like a spiritual power source to create an inner, peaceful silence, even while speaking with others in moments of stress or pressure. In fact, the shift from talking to speaking depends on the inner state we apply to the spoken word in a given moment. Talk is cheap; speaking is priceless.

A few weeks ago, I led a meditation at a retreat in Sedona, Arizona. One afternoon several days later, I hiked up Cathedral Rock, a famous Sedona landmark, with a few friends. It was my father's birthday, a gorgeous, sunny day, and as we climbed I reflected on my dad's life, work, and legacy. I had long been terrified of heights, and as we reached the top I knew he'd be so proud of me as I overcame fears and stretched in new directions. Suddenly, I heard a sound, turned around, and saw a man in traditional American Indian garb, sitting knees crossed, playing a flute, and looking over the mountain. My friend, who hiked this rock all the time, said she'd never seen anything like it. It was a perfect moment.

After a blissful half-hour or so on the summit, where we raised our faces to the sun to sit in stillness for a bit, my friends and I decided to descend. We could've spent the hike down in idle chit-chat. Instead, we wanted to hold on to the energy of that moment at the top for as long as humanly possible. So we elected to go down in silence. As we climbed down, my senses heightened, all thoughts vanished, and my soul poked its head out to absorb the natural beauty all around me. As we reached the bottom, I felt an extraordinary surge of power, serenity, and ease. I was alive.

Live Above the Law of Unnecessary Talk

When you feel the need to speak in a given situation, ask yourself three essential questions: Does it need to be said? Does it need to be said now? Does it need to be said by me? Surround yourself with people comfortable in serene silence and spend less time with loudmouths. Practice maintaining internal stillness while speaking and when you're required to present information in a work setting, say, strive not to identify as a client, employee, or boss. Divide your attention and try to speak from your soul. As you perfect this skill, you'll electrify your audience.

> Use the power you harness in stillness and silence to let your soul "eat" experiences, memories, and moments.

Use the power you harness in stillness and silence to let your soul "eat" experiences, memories, and moments. If you ever find yourself in a dark place in the future, you can access a memory you've sealed inside yourself and use it like a lamplight to guide you out. At times, the way out of darkness is kind of like the invisible platform 9¾ in the Harry Potter series. Harry uses the platform—only magical beings can see it—to board the train that takes him to another reality. In the same way, the stillness in you is a kind of invisible magic you can use to bring yourself back into the light.

Verification Point

Spend a Saturday in silence from the time you wake up until you fall asleep. You can grab a notepad to scribble on if you have to communicate for some reason. To be successful, you'll probably need to detox digitally, too, so no social media or email either. As you return to speaking the next day, notice the sound of your voice as you speak. Instead of endless small talk, ask conscious questions. For example: "What's one memory or experience that you think made you who you are today?" Use questions like this to elicit authenticity with your words.

31

THE LAW OF LYING

I used to lie to myself all the time. "I'm not a junkie," I'd think. "I'm just an artist!" Of course, you don't have to be a heroin addict to lie. We all do it. Some kinds of lies harm our spiritual growth, though. The ones we tell ourselves hurt us most, and lead to all other untruths. We tell white lies to make outer reality match our inner fictions, or we lie to a spiritual guide or coach, crippling our ability to consciously wake up. In order to live above the Law of Lying, we'll need to discard the kind of funhouse mirror image we may have of ourselves, and run headlong into reality.

The first kind of lie is the one we tell ourselves. These untruths corrode the foundation of our lives, as they skew our sense of ourselves, and warp our core values and desires. That dream you gave up on? "I didn't really

⬦⬦⬦⬦⬦⬦⬦⬦⬦⬦⬦⬦⬦⬦⬦⬦⬦⬦⬦⬦⬦

You may say to yourself, "Money is evil. I'm glad I'm broke. It's so freeing. I'm liberated." But you envy your wealthy friends and dream of future prosperity.

⬦⬦⬦⬦⬦⬦⬦⬦⬦⬦⬦⬦⬦⬦⬦⬦⬦⬦⬦⬦⬦

want it anyway," you may say, but it's all you think about. You may say to yourself, "Money is evil. I'm glad I'm broke. It's so freeing. I'm liberated." But you envy your wealthy friends and dream of future prosperity. Better yet: "I'm so spiritually evolved, I've ceased lying." Or you may force yourself to think, "I'm body positive. I love my body!" But you spend hours frustrated by the extra weight you're unable to shed. "I have forgiven anyone who has ever harmed me," you tell yourself, but you seethe with resentment.

All too often, tiny white lies—told daily, habitually—express externally the deeper ones we tell ourselves. You don't really work out, though you wish you did. But you went to Pilates one time, so when people ask what kind of workouts you do, you say, "Pilates." If you're late a lot, you arrive tardy to a wine tasting with friends and blame traffic because it's too painful to see you can't get where you want on time. In our tries to twist reality to escape seeing ourselves clearly, we seek to create an alternate one that spins make-believe stories about who we really are. This is dangerous, as it undercuts your ability to truly know yourself.

> A lie to a spiritual guide—a shaman, priest, or guru—is dangerous.

A lie to a spiritual guide—a shaman, priest, or guru—is dangerous, as well. For instance, let's say you're tasked to abstain from sex for ninety days to start to recover from a tumultuous relationship. A month or so in, you can't resist and sleep with someone. When you speak to your guru the next week, you make no mention. If he asks, you tell him you've maintained. This kind of lie can destroy us, for in doing so we short-circuit spiritual growth and ruin any chance of awakening. If you fall short in some area or break an agreement with your mentor, say it. Quickly. Be rigorously honest with spiritual guides. Otherwise, you'll feel confused and hopeless in a quest to awaken.

Like I said, when I lived the life of a literal junkie, I told myself so many lies. I spent my days taking long walks, drawing, and watching old films. Out at parties, though, when people asked me what I was up to, I managed to make it sound like I lived an incredibly fulfilling, hectic, busy week *because that's how I wanted to see myself.* I had worked so hard to cultivate this image that, eventually, I believed it myself.

◇◇◇◇◇◇◇◇◇◇◇◇◇◇◇◇◇◇◇◇◇◇◇◇◇◇◇◇
When I lived the life of a literal junkie, I told myself so many lies.
◇◇◇◇◇◇◇◇◇◇◇◇◇◇◇◇◇◇◇◇◇◇◇◇◇◇◇◇

One day, though, I walked into a Brooklyn bar at noon, went straight to the bathroom, and snorted a bag of heroin. Then I walked back out and ordered a whiskey. Typical Tuesday. It was a sunny day, and as light shined through the windows, I saw myself clearly for a bright, shining moment. The self-image I had worked so hard to construct fell apart, and I realized all of a sudden I really *was* the kind of person who spent Tuesday afternoons snorting heroin and drinking whiskey. I got sober for good soon after. Lies we tell ourselves don't last too long once exposed to light.

Live Above the Law of Lying

In order to live above the Law of Lying, start to observe when you tell white lies. Notice as you make excuses and bend facts to fit your self-image. In meditation, open yourself to see ideas you have about yourself that are inconsistent with verifiable reality. When engaged with a spiritual guide, practice radical honesty to get a granular level of clarity about who you are. Use a "set aside" prayer to ask: "God, please help me set aside all I think I know about myself, so I may have an open mind and a new experience. Please help me see truth."

Above this law, you no longer keep secrets from yourself. As a child, you kept them from yourself because you didn't want to see too clearly. You thought it would hurt too much. Now, as an adult, you can tackle the truth. The weird thing is, truth tastes terrible at first, but as it goes down, it has a wonderful bouquet, and leaves you feeling hearty and full. You can't live with your whole heart when you lie, especially to yourself.

Verification Point

Want to have some fun with this one? When you exaggerate, misrepresent, or flatly lie, pause, breathe, and tell on yourself. Tell whoever you're with, "You know what? I just lied." Then, explain what you lied about, and tell the truth. At first, this can be a bit brutal. Ultimately, though, it's a liberating exercise. I know, because I've done it!

32

THE LAW OF RECURRENCE

Along the horizontal line of reality, patterns recur. Baffled, we tend to cycle through the same situations on repeat. Breakups with the same kind of person over and over. Intense conflict with the same kind of boss. The same weight loss and weight gain on an on-again, off-again "diet." We may be aware of these patterns, but unsure how to break them. Under the law of recurrence, it's as if we circle the base of a tall mountain over and over, yearn to travel up toward the clouds and break the cycle, but can't quite figure out how to do it. Sound familiar? Well, let me show you how to climb.

First, though, we need to talk about what I call *resurrection addiction*. Yes, resurrection addiction. It's a thing. In this state, we tear ourselves down in self-destructive patterns so we can experience the thrill of building ourselves back up.

First, though, we need to talk about what I call *resurrection addiction*. Yes, resurrection addiction. It's a thing. In this state, we tear

154

ourselves down in self-destructive patterns so we can experience the thrill of building ourselves back up. In a sense, you're using drama, conflict, and pain to get "high" from the shocks they create. The quest to resurrect again and again is akin to the desire to be born anew. But it's misguided, as you're just arriving back to the same state on repeat.

The truth is, we're actually *choosing* to stay stuck in this cycle. Why? Well, in addition to the live-wire energy we generate from inner or interpersonal conflicts, the cycle is a familiar one. We're used to it, and in its comfort we find a way to self-medicate. It's scary to let go of what's familiar, even if it hurts us! But the root cause of our obsession with resurrection addiction is we don't know how to suck the same kind of energy from the vertical line, the one that will allow us to climb the spiritual mountain. Once we learn to use vertical line energy to climb, we'll revisit similar themes, but always from new and exciting vantage points.

> But the root cause of our obsession with resurrection addiction is we don't know how to suck the same kind of energy from the vertical line, the one that will allow us to climb the spiritual mountain.

Last year, I had an alcoholic client who desperately wanted to quit drinking. But she couldn't conceive of life without booze. Despite the hangovers, insomnia, and wrecked social life, she couldn't break the cycle. She'd obliterate herself at night, wake up, and start the process all over the next night. Rinse and repeat for years—you get the picture.

In spite of these struggles, though, she remained focused on a single morning years earlier. After a best-night-of-your-life kind of party, she walked up to her doorstep at six in the morning. Inside her white headphones, a U2 song—"Tryin' to Throw

Your Arms Around the World"—played softly. She took one look around her tree-lined street and thought, "Wow, perfect moment." As she relayed the story to me, she complained, "How will I ever feel that alive and free sober?"

So I showed her. I explained resurrection addiction, and that she was destroying herself to feel alive. I taught her how to achieve elevated states via intensive breathwork. I showed her how to create perfect moments via meditation using the same tools I laid out in earlier chapters. She grasped asking, and learned to make requests of the Divine in times of stress and discomfort. I also told her she needed to create spiritual experiences out in the world as exhilarating as the toxic ones that used to thrill her. So she went on a quest for exhilarating, sober experiences. She discovered ecstatic dance, meditative stargazing, and tantric sex. In other words, she found the thrill of life on the vertical line.

Live Above the Law of Recurrence

A predictable, routine meditative and asking practice is the key that unlocks the doorway to a life above this law. In fact, we really can't attain greatness without the feature of predictability. Even the wildest, craziest rock stars stick to tour schedules! In some ways, it may seem a little boring to live above the law of recurrence. At some point, you may even complain, "Where's the drama?" or "Where's the excitement?"

I recently heard an intriguing concept called "stability boredom," the idea being that some-

> "Stability boredom," the idea being that sometimes we see routine as a killer of spontaneity and thrill seeking.

times we see routine as a killer of spontaneity and thrill seeking. Nothing could be further from the truth. In fact, predictable routine is key to a rigorous spiritual practice. But an interior life lived on the vertical line is rich, vibrant, and thrilling. So the more black-and-white you make your spiritual routine—after all, you either meditated this morning or you didn't—the more your life starts to materialize in Technicolor. I promise you won't regret it.

Verification Point

Realize that you *choose* the patterns and cycles in your life. Ask yourself, "Am I aware that I actively choose this sequence of actions? Or am I asleep to the pattern?" When you find yourself at a familiar crossroads moment, start to use the words "I choose" out loud to make decisions. Say, "I choose to watch Netflix for nine hours," or "I choose to stay in a job I hate." See how that feels, and if it doesn't sit right, add new words after "I choose" to discover what you really want to do after all.

33

THE LAW OF DEATH

In the old fairy tale "Goldilocks and the Three Bears," our blond-haired heroine skips the too hot or too cold porridge, and the too small or too big chairs and beds. Instead, she finds the ones that that are "just right." Well, the way Goldilocks chooses the bears' stuff is exactly the way we want to choose to die. How? A too hot, active state of stress, excitement, and extremes doesn't work. Neither does a too cold, passive state of disinterest and surrender. We need to discover a "just right" present state: the soul's blissed-out neutrality. But we can't really predict when death will come, can we? So we need to cultivate this state every day we're alive.

In an active state, you freak out. A lot. Overscheduled, you overwork, and then brag about how busy you are. You fill your iCal till it glitches. You sip espressos till you can't sleep at night, then worry about that thing that happened today or the one that might happen tomorrow. All that stress strips away a sense of the present moment. Like the too hot or too cold porridge, it's a state of extremes. Do you really want to die like that?

In its lazy, bored apathy, a passive state isn't any better. Netflix queued, you eat Doritos and stare at your screen on a Tuesday evening. Or, you light candles, burn incense, and sculpt a perfect vision board. You never act on it. Thinking, "Oh, what's the use, anyway," you toss recyclables into the trash. Disinterested and ungrateful, you fail to appreciate the tiny miracles of daily life. Not a good state to leave this life in. Really, either state disables pure joy and keeps you from dying correctly.

> It must be true that we need death in order to fully experience life.

It must be true that we need death in order to fully experience life. Nearly all real-life shocks correlate to death, from risk-taking adventures to falling in love. The fresh and alive, fully present to all five senses moment after you've survived a near-fatal accident. The sharp sense of knowing, when you fall in love that one day you'll lose your beloved. Death can make life magical, as the closer we come to these risks, the more alive we feel. Death is the ultimate shock, the grand finale of shocks.

According to the Tibetan Book of the Dead, time runs forward as we live, but backward in the moment we die. As you die, you relive your entire life in reverse, arriving finally to the moment you're born. Then, you have a choice. Be free and move to a new plane of existence or relive your life over. When you die unconsciously, though, you don't have the needed power to choose. So, you repeat the life cycle again. Groundhog Day.

> Death can make life magical, as the closer we come to these risks, the more alive we feel.

But the one who lives a conscious death can choose, in this infant state, to break the cycle, and elevate to an ecstatic plane of being for eternity. The point of all effort to attain neutrality is to get into the conscious state that allows us to choose how we greet the moment of death. Dying in a neutral state, we have the choice to move to a higher level of experience. This is where our primary and secondary aims are leading. The point of these aims is to reach this state of neutrality.

In order to prepare yourself to die rightly while you're alive, you must choose to enter a neutral state as often as possible. To grasp what neutrality is, think of it this way: it's that fleeting moment where thoughts disappear, and you're fully alive to the present. Gaze into the eyes of your beloved. Float in the ocean on a perfect summer day. Play with a puppy. No cares. No worries. It is a moment of innocent trust in life, and that is a good state to die. Of course, it's also a good state to cultivate as a way of life.

For most of my life, I had a crippling fear of death. So I bit my nails till they bled and used meals to self-medicate, plying my little body with Chinese takeout or Girl Scout cookies to soothe overactive nerves. As I worked through this law, though, I shifted gears from neurotic to neutral. I meditated before meals, and then ate in silence. One evening, sitting in silence in front of a set table, I sobbed uncontrollably. In stillness, I realized that every time I'd tasted a meal since my mom died, I'd used the yummy taste of Mac 'n' Cheese or prosciutto sandwiches to dull the fear that I, too, could die at any moment. So my effort to eat intentionally led to a new discovery about my fear of dying.

Seeking to dissolve that fear and anger around my mom dying so young, I incorporated advanced breathwork and emotional release techniques into my morning practice. I sat in stillness, breathed in, then screamed and pounded the floor. As I detoxed off dense, dark feelings, I lay afterward in a state of complete bliss. One day, I noticed I'd stopped biting my nails, too! Once my fear of dying lifted, the habit just fell away.

I realized, too, I'd clutched too tightly to a stereotype witty, neurotic Jewish identity. If I shed death fear and anxiety, I imagined, I'd no longer belong to the club of whip-smart, witty Jews—Woody, Jerry, Groucho—I saw as my birthright. I'd lose my self, my very identity. You know what? I was right, in a way. As I let go of my fear of dying, I lost the neurotic parts of my personality, but kept the witty ones. Funnier now, my humor comes from a still, strong space inside me. It's more alive, more real. I still carry my cool kids crowd card, too. In the end, it turns out, when you become yourself, you belong everywhere.

Once I got comfy with my fear of dying, I started to wonder, 'Hmm . . . what's death actually like?' I'd been convinced dying was this terrifying, horrible thing, but I hadn't died, so I really had no idea. Instead of projecting scary visions onto this experience I know nothing about, why not come at death while I'm alive? Where I used to be paralyzed by anxieties around dying, now I floated above them, happy as a clam. I had reached neutrality, and I was ready for a conscious death.

Live Above the Law of Death

Arrive in a state of pure neutrality via a daily meditative and asking practice. Use self-observation via divided attention. Work with a spiritual teacher, too. These practices, though, are necessary but insufficient alone. Other paths to a neutral state lie in risk taking. Invite your partner into your wildest sexual fantasies. Allocate time to work on your dream project. Devote time to philanthropic causes. Strive to widen your circle of friends always. Travel as often as humanly possible. The thrill of an expansive life lived outside your comfort zone is a sure bet to shock you into the present.

Another way to neutrality entails an embrace of your emotions. Notice how you use buffers when anger and sadness arise. You may drink to numb feelings, overeat unhealthy foods to dull pain, or use intellectual analysis to wall off emotions. Instead of orbiting your feelings from a distance, lean into them. Sit and breathe through your nose, scream, cry, write. Whatever it takes to get to the pleasure of neutrality.

Verification Point

In your journal, write your eulogy. The one you dream will be delivered at your funeral. If you've ever delivered one, you know the form and style. If you haven't, Google "eulogy speech" for samples. This exercise is a powerful tool to get clear on the precious value of passing moments, hours, and days. It's like a compass rose you can use to determine the north star of your life, and see misalignment between your dreams and daily actions. Based on these gaps, you can then align what you do every day to your dreams, propelled by a new sense of urgency. As you write, play a piece of conscious music, perhaps something from the works of Hildegard von Bingen. Once you've written the talk, have a loved one read it aloud, or read it aloud yourself.

34

THE LAW OF THREE WISHES

When I was a kid, I used to play a game called "three wishes." The idea was that a magical genie would grant any three desires you listed, and the wishes were usually fairly standard: lots of money, a new car, big houses. Sometimes, an enlightened kid might cite world peace, or a clever one would shout, "unlimited wishes!" As adults we may be similarly childish, wishing for our dreams to materialize. But in his book *Self-Remembering*, Robert Earl Burton writes that if he had three wishes, he'd say only, "Thy will be done, thy will be done, thy will be done."

When I read Burton's book, this sentiment inspired me, because I realized there's really no other wish to be made. "But wait," you may say. "Doesn't this mean that I should get rid of all my own desires?" Not at all! Using life's wishes to ask for divine will to unfold at all times is a *co-creative* process. As long as you refine the mind and body to tune to the soul with a con-

> Using life's wishes to ask for divine will to unfold at all times is a *co-creative* process.

sistent spiritual practice, you will intuit useful desires aligned with the will of God. At the same time, unaligned wants will fall away over time. When you really live a life that's governed by divine will, your truest desires align with a kind of universal wisdom. So it's perfectly okay to *only* wish for divine, or universal, will to be done, *and* confidently pursue your aims at the same time.

> As long as you refine the mind and body to tune to the soul with a consistent spiritual practice, you will intuit useful desires aligned with the will of God.

The way some view "thy will be done" wishes, though, reminds me of a commonly told parable. Trapped by a flood on his rooftop, a man prayed to God for help. When a rescuer with a rowboat appeared, the man declined his help, saying, "No, I'll be fine. God will save me." Soon, a motorboat roared by, and its pilot offered rescue, but the man said, "No, I've prayed to God. He'll save me." Finally, a helicopter appeared, and a rope ladder dropped down onto the roof. "I'm fine, my faith in God will save me." After the man drowned, he went to Heaven and asked God, "Why didn't you save me?" God replied, "I sent you a rowboat, a motorboat, and a helicopter. What else did you expect?"

In the same way, sometimes we wish passively, thinking our destiny is going to simply show up. I've worked with single, lonely clients who refuse to date online, even though they want a partner, because they think it's not romantic. They want to discover a partner "naturally." But destiny doesn't work that way, and neither does divine will. As in the flood story, the universe serves up tools we can use to co-create our desires. In order to notice and use them properly, it helps to tune into this consciousness so we can hear what it's trying to say.

So, how do we use our wishes to co-create our lives? First, we need to listen. A lot. In the same way that you listen and speak in any conversation, start to listen (meditate) and speak (ask, or pray) to divine consciousness. It's like any relationship. When you meditate intently, over time brand-new intuitive thoughts and ideas will pop into your mind: "make this phone call, here's how to approach that conversation, reach out to your old friend." Often, these appear as images in the mind's eye, not actual words. Attuned to this deeper layer of consciousness, a prayerful and meditative human co-creates with divine power, shaping a life that she drives, and God powers.

Of course, as you strive to align desires with this supernaturally intelligent will, at times certain desires manifest in ways you don't anticipate or even want. An incredible career opportunity arrives, but it's not quite the one you had envisioned. You fall in love with a different kind of person than the one you visualized in meditation. In these moments, it's vital to trust that sometimes divine will is leading you, in fits and starts, to a life *beyond* your wildest dreams: experiences and results you couldn't have conceived of that fulfill you in ways you never even thought possible.

I used to want to look like a rail-thin, waifish runway model. I deprived myself of meals, took hot yoga classes obsessively, and snorted heroin as a weight loss strategy. One night, my friend Kal, who owned the nightclub where I deejayed, said to me, "What's really annoying about you, Biet, is you're fucking perfect, but you're trying to have someone else's body. The guy who's going to love *you* wants a woman with a big, bodacious ass."

In other words, my obsession with skinniness was distorting the kinds of men I attracted. As I got sober and cultivated a meditative practice, this deeply held, unaligned desire fell away, and I got super comfy with my curvy body. Sure enough, I fell in love with a man who happens to love me as I am—a petite, curvy brunette. In fact, he doesn't really find super-skinny women attractive. If I had somehow succeeded in my unaligned desire to stay rail-thin, I might have missed out on my best friend!

Live Above the Law of Three Wishes

Start to spend as much time as possible tuned to divine consciousness. Befriend all events life serves you, mindful of the mantra, "Thy will be done." Developing an optimistic relationship to all that takes place today is always a winning strategy. To tap into this consciousness, imagine two radio stations. Your mind is typically tuned to self-will radio: fuzzy, noisy, loud. But it's been on in the background for so long, you can barely even hear it any longer.

In order to tune into universal mind, you need to tune into consciousness radio. Through the process of sitting and listening, you'll start to hear calm, new intuitive thoughts, and bold ideas. As time goes on, you'll notice that the actions you take from this layer of consciousness tend to feel easy and effective, where before, tuned into self-will radio, they felt choppy, anxious, and difficult.

Verification Point

Start to recite "Thy will be done" as many times a day as you wish. You can also use "Your will be done" if it feels more modern! When disturbed or out of sorts, use this wish as a kind of mantra. The tool is especially effective in moments of conflict. You can be in a heated argument, or have someone literally yelling in your face, and when you recite the mantra in your mind, it will bring tranquillity and compassion, making you more effective in a stressful moment.

THE LAW OF IMAGINATION

Maybe the greatest imaginer of all time, Leonardo da Vinci, sketched prototypes for the helicopter, parachute, and battle tank, made massive breakthroughs in fields from paleontology to architecture, and painted some of the most famous masterpieces on the planet, like the *Mona Lisa*. So, imagination is great, right? Well, yes! But in one of his many notebooks, he also wrote, "The man who is not aware of his mistakes cannot correct them." His words present a key problem we face under this law. When we substitute imagination for reality, we can't see our flaws and mistakes. Misused, the gift of imagination leads us to worry, fantasize, and ruminate. Freed from misuse, though, you can be like Leo. You might not paint the *Mona Lisa*, but you can use your gift to dare greatly.

All too often, imagination takes you for a ride you don't want to go on. You get one text message from that guy you talked to at the party, and start to plan the wedding. Then you never hear from him again. It hurts. Out to coffee with a friend, you share a vulnerable secret, and you think she looked at you funny. You inner consider. You obsess about it for days. It consumes your thoughts. You ask her about it, and she asks, "What are you talking about?" We fantasize or worry about imagined scenarios, and both harm us equally. The misuse of imagination is like stepping onto a terrifying roller coaster you don't really want to ride.

At times, we imagine in order to avoid seeing ourselves as we are. You may think of yourself as super-healthy and gluten-free, and when out with friends at a restaurant, you order a pristine plate. At home, though, you eat a pint of ice cream or order pizza in your pajamas. Nothing wrong with that! But if you see yourself as the healthiest eater around, and conveniently ignore the late night pint, you might scoff at others' bad eating habits, or boast about your imagined perfect choices. In this way, imagination can lead to a kind of distorted vanity. In fact, it's actually dangerous to ascribe to yourself traits you don't have. You need to see yourself clearly to build the life of your dreams.

If you don't, you can cause long-lasting damage. Years ago, my father came up with an off the wall thought experiment to illustrate this law. Imagine a group of girls with moms addicted to crack cocaine. Some of these moms tell their daughters, "I love you, baby. You are everything to me." Yet they live the self-destructive, abusive lifestyle that comes along with serious drug addiction. Lying to themselves, they imagine that they parent in a loving way. The other moms aren't in imagination, though. They tell their kids, "I don't give a shit about you, the only thing I care about is crack," and keep smoking.

As the years pass, the girls whose moms say, "I love you, you're everything to me" become drug addicts, confusing love with drug addiction. The other women, whose mothers said, "I don't care about you" become stable, responsible adults, and live drug-free lives. The first group of moms was in imagination, so their kids were as well. The second group of moms set their kids free, in a sense, because they never confused love with drug addiction. This is precisely what is meant in the Gospel of John: "Then you will know the truth, and the truth will set you free."

Live Above the Law of Imagination

Set yourself free. Observe when you go into imagination, and start to tell fantasy from reality. If you start to notice yourself slipping into misuse of your gift, ask yourself, "Do I have any verifiable facts to back my thinking right now?" Watch out for lies, omissions, and exaggerations designed to protect your self-image, and practice saying what's true. Also, stop trying to shape others' perceptions of you, and own your emotional states. If you feel like shit, say so. It may be uncomfortable, even painful at first, but this clear-eyed of view of reality is a wellspring of personal power.

> It may be uncomfortable, even painful at first, but this clear-eyed of view of reality is a wellspring of personal power.

Until you let go of the person you imagine yourself to be, you'll never be the person you want to become. It's really that simple. So, during your morning practice, ask to see the truth about yourself, and situations and challenges you may face. You can say, "Please show me the truth about . . ." Ask a lot. It works if you do it! Misused imagination

> *Until you let go of the person you imagine yourself to be, you'll never be the person you want to become.*

can only survive as long as you think it's real. In order to live above The Law of Imagination, we need to find and let go of patterns of thinking where a gap exists between our perception and verifiable reality.

Verification Point

For this verification, start to use your imagination so that it doesn't use you. Select an area in your life where you'd like to apply the power of your imagination, like a relationship, personal wellness, or your career. You may be single, but you want a partner and children, for example. Ask for calm and peace to accept that you're not where you'd like to be in this area yet. Then, as you meditate, imagine this desire fully realized. Use your senses to visualize vivid details. How do you feel in this new state? What do you see? In your journal, describe this fulfilled desire you visualized in meditation. Use your five senses to paint a vivid portrait of what it would feel like to realize this desire. Then, use this sensory vision to inspire yourself to pursue what you want!

36

THE LAW OF THE FOUR CENTERS

"My emotions got the best of me." "My instincts took over." You've probably heard the words countless times. These clichés try to explain phenomena we can't quite grasp. What they're really trying to do, though, is explain one of the human centers seemingly running on its own power. In the work I study, humans hold four distinct centers—separate compartments of our being. Emotional. Intellectual. Instinctive. Movement. Left unchecked, each center acts on its own, trying to run our lives in its own unique way. Once we grasp the proper use of each one, though, we can deploy them to govern our lives and master our being.

In the emotional center, states of being tend to run fast, hot, and volatile. Infatuated, for example, we can fall head over heels in love quite quickly. This center races past all others, reacting swiftly to perceived slights. It's the unhinged Queen of Hearts in *Alice in Wonderland*, who shouts angrily, "Off with his head!" or "Off with her head!" When unrefined, emotionally centered humans can be a destructive force of nature; impulsive moves, hissy fits, and freak-outs are its baser tendencies. It is also, of course, the center through which we shed cathartic tears, sense appreciation, and bliss out on lovers, family, and friends.

A key point: the emotional center is a kind of *supernatural power* that can lead us to awaken. In fact, a conscious wake up is most readily available via the emotional center. All four centers need to align in us, and each plays its part, but the emotional state leads the way. You can think of it as a kind of first among equals. Since this center is the speediest, and we don't have infinite time to awaken on this planet, it's vital to leverage emotional states to rapidly boost ourselves to a state of presence. To reach nirvana, you're going to need to rely on this center most.

> The emotional center is a kind of *supernatural power* that can lead us to awaken.

The intellectual center fosters critical thought and tends to move slowly via methodical analysis. The seat of curiosity and wisdom, the intellect absorbs and retains knowledge. With a slow, methodical pace, intellectually centered humans tend to respond thoughtfully, not reactively. Though *we can't access enlightenment via this center*, spiritual concepts and ideas have to be laundered through the intellect to make them clear, and relatable. The intellectual center sure as shit processed this book, though its roots lie in the spiritual realm via lived emotional experiences. Because the intellect views reality in terms of solving problems, it tends to ruminate or move into analysis paralysis when no rational solution appears.

The instinctive center—the one that keeps us alive on the planet—houses the intuitive faculties. It's the sense that you shouldn't walk down that dark alley or put your hand into the campfire. You don't need a rational explanation. You just know. Instinctively centered humans like to focus on physical comforts or necessities like temperatures, lighting, and food supplies. Moms of all kinds generally tend to feature this center. With a strong instinctive center, you'll be super safe and assess risk quickly, but you may also be prone to neurosis and worry. Though instincts are essential to survival, we need to use the other centers to neutralize overly instinctive behavior, as it can lead to a survival mode way of thinking and make us overly fearful.

The movement center deploys a range of motion, as well as the use of our senses. Obviously, whenever we run, dance, or cycle, we're using this center. Yogis, ballet dancers, and gymnasts operate primarily from movement, as well as many actors. But the moving center is also the playground of architects and cartoonists, as it heavily relies on sight. In their use of touch, massage therapists are moving-centered as well. Visually oriented and attentive to seeing spatially, moving centered humans can see a building or drawing in a space before it's realized. When we move our hands to write, as in a journal entry, we use our movement center to create a visual representation of thoughts and ideas.

Live Above the Law of the Four Centers

Start to apply the appropriate center for a given moment. If you have to wake up super-early for work or a flight, for example, your instinctive center will tend to dominate. Your eyes may hurt. You may feel groggy. Your body may ache a bit. Use this moment as an opportunity to shift into the emotional center. Focus on gratitude—for your morning coffee, the modern gift of flight, or work you enjoy. Considering a long-term relationship? It may sound counterintuitive, but you need to use the intellect to make clear-eyed decisions in romance, discerning whether your interests, visions, and plans align. Look to choose the appropriate center in response to situations you face each day.

Start to use the supernatural power of the emotional center to awaken. Run headlong *into* pain, and begin to see rage, sadness, or fear as fertile soil for spiritual growth. Especially when you're caught up in these states, use your meditation toolkit to alchemize emotions into an elevated state. Ask for clarity, and breathe in through your nose, then exhale deep into the diaphragm. Feel a tingling in the nerve centers of your foot, and know your body is receiving your intentional messages.

> Run headlong *into* pain, and begin to see rage, sadness, or fear as fertile soil for spiritual growth.

Verification Point

Observe yourself when troubled, and ask, "Am I using the right center for this moment?" For example, do you get angry when you receive constructive feedback on your ideas at work? You're using the emotional center in a setting suited to the intellect. Pause, breathe deeply, and use the intellectual center to respond. If a lover says, "I love you," and you respond with a cold, "Thanks," you're using the intellectual center in a moment that calls for emotion. Instead, use the emotional center to respond warmly. A misuse of the moving center is to endlessly tap your leg when you're anxious. Instead, you can use the intellectual center to know you're safe, and use the moment as an opportunity to breathe and meditate. When a friend asks how you're doing, a natural response is to use the instinctive center to stay safe: "I'm great!" You can use the vulnerability of the emotional center to respond openly and share about what's really going on inside. Note which center you deploy most often, and see where you may be trying to fit a square peg into a round hole.

37

THE LAW OF IMPOSTERS

Humpty Dumpty sat on a wall. Humpty Dumpty had a great fall. All the king's horses and all the king's men, couldn't put Humpty together again." A classic nursery rhyme, sure, but a powerful lesson, too. As infants, we arrive on the planet in a pure soul state, a unified essence. As we grow older, we accrue notions about "the way things are" from parents, teachers, or friends that often oppose or contradict each other. As our "self" fractures into warring pieces, at some point we shatter and have a great fall. Then, as adults, we may look to others—therapists, partners, coaches—to put us back together, and sometimes it seems like they just can't.

Imposters manifest as stray thoughts and beliefs that aren't ours, as ideas we've picked up along the way at some point in our lives. Think about it this way. If a houseguest inadvertently left her iPhone at your home, it's unlikely you'd say to yourself, "Great, I've been wanting the new one!" But this is how we often function in relation to our imposters. We say to ourselves, "Well, that's my thought, so it must be *me*." Wrong. It's like your friend's iPhone, an item plopped into your mind by an outside entity, and claimed by you now as your own.

There are many entirely separate expressions of "you." Imposters are strong, and they can pull you in seemingly opposite directions. For example, one of you really likes to go shopping at Barneys, and wants new handbags and clothing every season. But another "you" thinks you should renounce materialism, move to the mountains, and join an ashram. In this case, what is authentic and what is an imposter?

If you enjoy the feel of quality fabrics, express your artistic viewpoint via fashion, and feel a sense of ease and calm as you shop, it's an authentic choice. If you buy clothes to run away from yourself, you're led by an imposter. Same with the ashram. If your quest leads you to a community away from modern society, where you experience a calm kind of neutrality, the choice is in essence. If you're moving to the mountains in a vain attempt to avoid life, you'll usually worry and feel anxiety as an imposter runs the show.

The biggest problem with imposters is we don't know they exist! To expel them, you first have to recognize them. Living under imposters, you may often feel indecisive, or you may experience tremendous highs and low lows. You may feel confused or ashamed, like you're living a lie, because you're trying to juggle the many imposters vying for mastery of your being. You may often experience unpleasant thoughts or emotions, as you identify imposter thoughts and beliefs as your own. The imposter will cause you to think about yourself too often, leading to worry, guilt, and frustration.

Through meditative practices, you can identify and eject imposters. If you struggle to discern whether a thought, idea, or belief is an imposter, here's a litmus test: Does it calm you? Does it fill you with joy? Or, does it provoke anxiety, worry, or fear? If it's the latter, it's an imposter. Our essence—the soul—is a state of pure bliss and love, and thoughts that emanate from this space empower and strengthen us. Any idea or belief that tears us down, makes us feel insignificant, or tells us we're unworthy is an imposter.

> Our essence—the soul—is a state of pure bliss and love, and thoughts that emanate from this space empower and strengthen us.

To grasp this law, consider a metaphor. Imagine, for a moment, a woman who owns a great mansion, employing many servants. Busy with other priorities, she disappears for long stretches of time. After a year away, she returns to find the mansion in disrepair, broken down, and dysfunctional. The servants have become lazy, unproductive, and frivolous. Like the woman with a mansion, the soul needs to govern all aspects of the personality, including imposters, if we want our lives to make sense. When we neglect the soul, though, our lives become chaotic and messy. In the same way the mansion needs an owner to tell the servants what to do in order to operate effectively, a human needs the soul to govern over imposters in order to function effectively, as well.

Live Above the Law of Imposters

So, the soul needs to be a badass boss when it comes to imposters. How do we put the innocent soul in charge of strong imposters? Of course, a daily meditation practice is essential. But you need to harness the strength of all these imposters, and govern them. Above this law, imposters do *your* bidding. So, you shop at Barneys *and* you spend weeks on an ashram. With your soul in the driver's seat, you do whatever you want. In this authentic state, you harmonize your imposters and live a unified life.

This is what Jesus meant when he said, "Get behind me, Satan." You want your imposters behind you, while you lead them from the front, and the only way to do this is to remember yourself. The real you doesn't have doubt or fear. How could it, when it only exists in this moment? In this space of now, the real you is relaxed, effective, and impressively alive. The more you live from this space, the more you will forgive anyone who ever helped plant an imposter in your mind.

◇◇◇◇◇◇◇◇◇◇◇◇◇◇◇◇◇◇◇◇◇◇

With your soul in the driver's seat, you do whatever you want.

◇◇◇◇◇◇◇◇◇◇◇◇◇◇◇◇◇◇◇◇◇◇

Verification Point

Note the number of times you say "I" in a day. If you'd like, you can gently pinch your wrist when you do as a reminder. Pause, and ask yourself, "Is this coming from *me*, or is this the work of an imposter?" It doesn't matter how many times you say "I," or whether your statements are authentic or not. But begin to notice how often you may state beliefs or thoughts that don't express the real you, or suppress the love and bliss of the soul. Just as it's impossible to see a clear reflection on the surface of a pond filled with ripples, we can't see ourselves clearly until we start to locate our imposters.

38

THE LAW OF PAIN

Back when I was a junkie, I snorted heroin to kill painful feelings. Since I got sober, I've tried to do the same with everything from sex to bagels. Let me tell you, it doesn't work. You can't kill the soul, either—though it can fall asleep for a time—as it's immortal, indestructible even. Unlike the ephemeral body and mind, it is never born and never dying. Rooted in the emotional center, pain is somewhat similar, and never ceases while we're alive. You can try to numb it, deny it, or shame it, but it's actually fertile soil you can use to plant and grow a new you.

Naively, I used to think that one day I could eliminate all my pain via spiritual practice. Over time, though, I realized that enlightenment doesn't render you clean as the driven snow. Trying to get rid of pain is like trying to strip colors from a rainbow. Can you imagine a rainbow without red, blue, or green? Pain and grief color you beautifully, rendering your whole humanity with texture and depth. In fact, I feel most awake when I embrace all my flaws, anger, and sadness. In no scenario does an awake life turn us into happiness robots. If you encounter anyone who suggests it does, run away!

I used to think that if someone was enlightened, then they were perfect, too. Not true! As a bit of a perfectionist myself, though, I thought I shouldn't reveal pains and flaws. In my mind, I needed to show up as a perfect spirit at all times. What I didn't realize at the time is I was denying myself energy. In fact, trying to hide pain is just another way to try to kill it. Sharing it with others can energize you, in the same way a plant photosynthesizes sunlight. Eventually, I got it: God doesn't speak through perfect mes-

> Eventually, I got it: God doesn't speak through perfect messengers. The more pain I reveal, the more human I am. The more human I am, the more connected I am to everyone around me.

sengers. The more pain I reveal, the more human I am. The more human I am, the more connected I am to everyone around me.

Last summer, I heard the story of Immaculée Ilibagiza, a Tutsi survivor of the Rwandan genocide. Hidden in a priest's home, she lived in a three-foot-by-four-foot bathroom with several other women for three months, while nearly a million Tutsis were killed across the country. A devout Catholic, she tried to recite the Lord's Prayer, the one that begins, "'Our Father . . .'" But when she reached the line that states, "'as we forgive those who trespass against us,'" she paused. She simply couldn't recite the line.

You see, Hutus had killed almost her entire family, and she was filled with an all-consuming rage. Her heart hated, as she indulged fantasies where she brutally killed these killers. In our terms, she was trying to quell pain with rage, hatred, and murderous fantasy. Nevertheless, she persisted in prayer, reciting her self-edited "Our Father." One day it dawned on her: "Who am I to edit the Lord's Prayer?" She realized God would never author a prayer that needed editing.

As she spoke the prayer aloud, unedited, thousands of times, she penetrated that elusive line on forgiveness. Suddenly a white light surrounded her, and she felt like she was floating. Forgiveness flooded her heart, as she realized her family's Hutu torturers already lived in the most real hell imaginable, the one they had made for themselves. Via prayer, she transmuted excruciating pain into spiritual transformation.

As peace returned to Rwanda, she even visited one of her family's killers in prison. In her book *Left to Tell*, she writes, "I wept at the sight of his suffering." Then, she reached out, touched his hand, and said, "I forgive you." When a shocked jailer asked how she could possibly forgive the man who killed her mother and brother, she responded, "Forgiveness is all I have to offer." Armed with the power of forgiveness, she authored a best-selling book, launched a charitable foundation, and now inspires audiences across the globe with her powerful message of forgiveness.

> You can't kill pain, but you *can* leverage it to grow spiritually.

Via prayer, she discovered treasure in a horrifying tragedy. Immaculée had tried to kill her grief with revenge fantasies, fury, and hatred. It didn't work, as it never does. In her use of prayer, or asking, though, she was able to transmute pain into personal transformation. She not only healed, but also lighted a path for others to use asking pain as a tool to wake up. You can't kill pain, but you *can* leverage it to grow spiritually.

Live Above the Law of Pain

In order to live above the Law of Pain, start to redefine vulnerability as a key source of strength. Begin to see that tears and sorrow are a language of the soul, just like bliss and tranquillity. So, cease to orbit your pain by trying to hide it with hatred or shame.

Instead, unbox and reveal it to a trusted guide, close friend, or even yourself. Processed pain resides in bliss, so if you try to avoid the former, you close access to the latter. Look at what Immaculée's vulnerable gift created out of unspeakable tragedy!

> Pain resides in bliss, so if you try to avoid the former, you close access to the latter.

I want to be clear, though. What this *doesn't* mean is awkwardly speaking openly about pain without any attempt to grow and change via asking. If it still sounds like a sob story, you're not *in* the pain at all; you're orbiting it like a tourist. Though this kind of hopeless openness may mask as vulnerability, it's a kissing cousin to whines and complaints. It doesn't create energy; it drains us down. Rather, wear pain openly with dignity and joy, confident in a meditative practice that transmutes grief into gold. The meditative life is one of limitless expansion!

> Wear pain openly with dignity and joy, confident in a meditative practice that transmutes grief into gold.

Verification Point

Use tiny pains to practice transmuting pain into bliss. When you stub your toe hard, imagine that feeling as blissful. Outdoors in winter and bitter cold wind blows on your face? Notice how the crisp air makes you feel alive. Play around with these pain/bliss dynamics to get a sense for how the sensations are similar. Use this new idea to start alchemizing pain into bliss.

39

THE LAW OF DUALITY

The abstract painter Agnes Martin used to hang a little sign on her mirror that read, "You're wrong!" The first words she saw every morning, the sign helped her remember that, whatever took place on a daily basis, her first take on an event was often off base. Agnes was on to something. In my view, her little sign was an attempt to live above the law of duality. Under this law, our thinking is literal and inside the box, as the dualistic mind likes to think in either/or terms. Pain is bad. Pleasure is good. "I didn't land the deal. That's bad," or "I landed the deal. That's good." To live above duality, we're going to need to free our minds of this kind of black-and-white thinking.

In fact, life is a sequence of contradiction and paradox. Under a dualistic mind-set, we can't possibly grasp that pain is priceless. Chemotherapy is lethal, but it can kill cancer and give life. We can literally touch God

> Once we experience meditative bliss, we discover it's what we wanted all along.

consciousness in meditation, but we resist the practice fiercely. Once we experience meditative bliss, we discover it's what we wanted all along, but the next day resistance returns, and we repeat the cycle. We fear death, but it's the very fact that life is lived against a ticking clock that makes it so valuable. To the literal, either/or mind, none of this makes any sense.

Black-and-white thinking is a confidence killer, too. This mind-set doesn't anticipate intervals à la the Law of Seven, because it assumes that life *should* always unfold smoothly. A person living with this mind state will therefore be unable to handle denying force. He may quit, or give up at the first sign of difficulty. You see, dualist thought presents a kind of conditional confidence, and it relies on friction-free forward momentum. As soon as obstacles and roadblocks emerge, the confident facade falters and breaks. Under this law, we may say to ourselves, "I can't withstand *that*," or "This is what always happens to me." Here, we fail to see how challenges purify and sculpt us into higher states, refining us as awakened beings. Instead, most people wait twenty years to discover, in hindsight, "Oh, *that's* why it played out that way," or, "I really should have gone for it after all."

Dualistic thought leads to so much regret. Under it, we can't see that taking risks and stretching outside comfort zones is the key to expansion. Instead, this law lulls us to sleep by telling us status quo comfort is the key to happiness. So we stay stuck, seeking lives of comfort and safety. It makes sense, right? Growth hurts. Risks are scary. We might fail! Mark Twain said it best, so I'll let him take it away: "Twenty years from now you will be more disappointed by the things you didn't do than by the ones you did do. So throw off the bowlines. Sail away from the safe harbor. Catch the trade winds in your sails. Explore. Dream. Discover." Sounds like an incredible way to live! In dualistic thought, though, you can't be adventurous like that. You won't be safe enough.

An ancient Chinese parable shows us how to start to live above this mind-set. It starts like this: A farmer and his son had a prized stallion that helped the two men earn a living. One late summer day, the horse ran away. Soon after, neighbors from a nearby village visited to offer condolences. "What a shame," they said. "Your only horse is gone. How unfortunate you are! What terrible luck! How will you live, prosper, and work the land?" The farmer replied only, "We'll see."

A few days later, the horse returned, leading a few wild mares behind him. Word of the farmer's good fortune got out in the village, and the neighbors visited again, saying, "What great luck! You must be so happy!" The farmer replied, "We'll see." The next morning, the farmer's son tried to train the wild horses, but one of the mares threw him to the ground, breaking his leg. The villagers cried, "Your son broke his leg, what terrible luck!" The farmer replied only, "We'll see."

A few weeks later, war broke out, and soldiers from the Emperor's army marched through town, recruiting all able-bodied boys. They did not take the farmer's son, deemed unfit because of his broken leg. Friends shouted, "Your boy is spared, what tremendous luck! You must be so happy!" The farmer replied only, "We'll see."

As you can see, the farmer lived above the idea that any one event was ever "good" or "bad," and was never certain any event had a specific meaning. Like the Greek philosopher Epictetus, he understood that it was "his business to manage carefully and dexterously whatever happens." In his neutral state, the farmer was free from the ups and downs of daily life. As so many of us are addicted to and trapped by this roller-coaster cycle every day, we would do well to take a page from the farmer's playbook.

Live Above the Law of Duality

Like the farmer, realize you don't always know what's "good" or "bad" in your life. In other words, sometimes, well, you're wrong! It's your spiritual duty to turn and seek second opinions, or at least get curious about other points of view. So, start to see the treasure in your tragedies in the present moment, rather than in hindsight or on reflection. Cultivate the belief that you live in a benevolent universe, that all things unfold as they should. When difficulty arises, ask yourself, "In what ways is this good? How can I grow and benefit here? How can I even *enjoy* this difficulty?" When you run into a roadblock, notice a tendency to give up. Instead, be flexible. Pursue other routes and new approaches to a goal, remaining confident in your vision.

> Start to see the treasure in your tragedies in the present moment, rather than in hindsight or on reflection.

> Cultivate the belief that you live in a benevolent universe, that all things unfold as they should.

Verification Point

Select an experience you've endured that you see as terrible. Look to see what valuable treasures you stored as a result of this tragedy or mishap. In your journal, describe the treasures you dug up via an experience you see as harmful or tragic. See what attributes you now possess as a result of a challenging experience. Dig deep, take the exercise into meditation, and ask to see the truth. If you cannot see yet what the treasure or gift was in this incident, use the tool of asking for it to be revealed to you. As you do so, think of qualities you may have acquired, such as resilience, courage, tolerance, or patience. Next, select one dream you hold for the future. Ask yourself, "Is it *possible* that this dream will still happen despite this event from my past?" If the answer is "yes," congrats! You're living above this law right now. If "no," recognize you're trapped in dualistic thinking. Ask to see what is blocking you. Say, "God, please help me see this situation as you see it. Show me your endless possibility."

40

THE LAW OF THE BODY

I used to spend all my time way up on the vertical line of reality, my head in the clouds, dreaming of the spiritual. I spoke unique ideas, thought novel thoughts, and fascinated friends at fancy parties, as most humans talk and think about, well, normal stuff. Life on the vertical line fascinated me, too; it's pretty interesting up there! As an artist, I saw myself as uniquely aware, apart from and above boring physical reality. But as the Catholic monk Thomas Merton writes, the artist's authenticity lifts him "above the level of the world without delivering him from it." Eventually, I crashed down to earth.

> I used to spend all my time way up on the vertical line of reality, my head in the clouds, dreaming of the spiritual.

How did I crash? Well, I realized that all that time up on the vertical line, I was just trying to escape the reality that my body was going to die. You see, I associated my organs, bones, and blood with a material world I kind of hated. Wars. Famine. Disease. So, I kind of hated my body, too. I hated its flaws and weaknesses. I also knew I'd leave it someday, so I tossed my body into the same mental category as all the other things I'd leave behind when I died—friends, family, flowers, fluffy cats.

Happily, I discovered why I tried to put space between my body and me. It scared me to lose such a precious gift, to part with it at death, this temple that holds celestial, mystical truths. It was unthinkable, nearly unbearable. But I found a solution. When I consciously chose to accept that my body would die, I could truly love myself. Tiny height. Voluptuous thighs. Snotty colds. All of it.

Under the Law of the Body, you may try to fly away from the present moment in regret and worry: "I'm going to fail." "I shouldn't have eaten that ice cream last night." "No one will ever love me." "That was such a stupid mistake." As you escape into thinking about the past or future, you're really trying to abandon yourself. But if anyone else talked to you the way you often talk to yourself, you'd never stand for it! You may wonder why you do it, then. It's possible you're trying to avoid the heartbreak you'll feel when you die and lose the precious gift of yourself.

> As you escape into thinking about the past or future, you're really trying to abandon yourself.

But why would anyone do that? Well, when you love your talents, your gifts, and the face you see in the mirror, your sense of responsibility for your life on this planet skyrockets. Naturally, you love others, live a fulfilled life, and build a community. But, as they say, you can't take it with you when you go. Inevitably, in spite of this love and all you've created, you're going to lose it all the day you die. All of it. How is that not sad, right? So, to spare yourself the pain of losing such valuable treasure, you

So, to spare yourself the pain of losing such valuable treasure, you choose mediocrity, safe and protected by your average life when you die.

choose mediocrity, safe and protected by your average life when you die.

The process is similar to the way some people resist the risk of realizing true love: they're afraid someday they'll lose it. In Bob Dylan's "Like a Rolling Stone," he sings, "When you ain't got nothing, you got nothing to lose." Believe me, I get it. That's why commitment phobes don't commit! They know the best-case love story scenario ends with two true loves holding ninety-year-old hands on a deathbed. But really, that's the point. We're meant to lose it all, and that loss is a moment of pure beauty, not grim death.

Around eight years ago, when I had been sober for a few months, I was walking down a crooked West Village street. I passed by a townhome, and through a large window, I saw a family Christmas party, with red and green lights, sweaters, cider, the whole bit. I stopped in my tracks, and looking through the window, I wondered how I could be so poor and unhappy in the midst of so much prosperity and joy.

Then it hit me. I wasn't allowing myself to even *try* to become wealthy because I was too scared to part with prosperity when I died. Subconsciously, I guess I figured it'd be easier to part with, well, poverty and misery. Over time, I realized in fact, this was a cruel lie. In fact, the more I desire, the more I gain. The more I gain, the more I give. It may sound strange, but it was a courageous act to make money for me. I knew it was my duty! It was then that I harnessed the courage to finally be willing to lose so much when I died.

Live Above the Law of the Body

To live above this law, you need to be in the present moment. There's a reason it's called the "present," right? It's a gift! So, start to practice *being* here, where your feet are, where your body is, at all times. When you're sad or upset, notice that your first instinct may be to run away into your mind, with its anxieties and fears. Instead, choose to stay present in your body and let emotions wash over you. Practice stillness, and let it be. Pledge to treat your body with love, and make it as healthy as you can, in spite of the fact that you will lose it to a great, shocking breakup one day.

◇◇◇◇◇◇◇◇◇◇◇◇◇◇◇◇◇◇◇◇◇◇◇◇◇◇◇◇

There's a reason it's called the "present," right? It's a gift!

◇◇◇◇◇◇◇◇◇◇◇◇◇◇◇◇◇◇◇◇◇◇◇◇◇◇◇◇

Verification Point

Use a body scan meditation to observe your body from head to toe. Let your eyelids relax, and your eyes close. Allow your tongue to fall back into your mouth. Let your shoulders relax. Notice a knot of nervous tension in the stomach. Breathe deeply into the diaphragm through your nose, and then exhale. As you scan, ask, "What do I sense in my body?" Observe if a sensation, say, in your stomach, is tied to an emotion. If so, practice being with that feeling, and breathe into it.

41

THE LAW OF BEHOLDING

Imagine that the universe is like a giant projector, and its only job is to project a blissful film onto the screen of your life. Trials and triumphs. Sorrows and joys. In this scenario, you can either be a blank canvas that receives and holds this life story, or you can step in front of the projector, making silly shadow puppets that you think tell a better one. It's counterintuitive, but in order to create yourself, you need to step aside and let the universe do the heavy lifting to sculpt you into the being the universe, or God, intends. It's so much easier!

> Imagine that the universe is like a giant projector, and its only job is to project a blissful film onto the screen of your life.

Some humans get in the way of this projector, distorting the image. In other words, they get in the way of the ideal vision the universe holds for their own lives. What does this look like in practice? In the Dalai Lama's words, it's the man who, for example, "sacrifices his health in order to make money. Then he sacrifices money to recuperate his health. And then he is so anxious about the future that he does not enjoy the present." In other words, we're *trying* too hard to get what we want, rather than trusting in divine conscious- ness. The result? We're confused, chaotic, obstructed.

In this state, we toss obstacles into our own path, making our lives more difficult with each step. Sometimes, the solutions we develop are worse than the original problem. We get into horrible relationships to escape loneliness, develop workaholic tenden- cies to prove our own value to the world, or use credit cards to get out of debt. Anxiety, frustration, and fear flow from these self-propelled "solutions." Trying to control our lives, we hold the reins too tightly, and turn our lifelong dreams into near night- mares.

> Sometimes, the solutions we develop are worse than the original problem.

On the other hand, those who create themselves weave them- selves seamlessly into the film the universe projects. As they suck the marrow out of life, plunging headlong into a role as the hero of their own story, they create themselves as a beholder. To behold life fully without standing in the way of its inception is to allow yourself to be created. In other words, we create ourselves by first stepping aside. Via divided attention, we're able to both behold the universe's vision of our highest selves, and use the en- ergy of that insight to author the story of our own lives.

The aim is to be a trans- lucent space where magical shit seems to happen end- lessly. When someone is in a state of beholding, they see your highest possibility.

> To behold life fully without standing in the way of its inception is to allow yourself to be created.

They want you to realize it even more than you want it for yourself. Think Robin Williams in *Dead Poets Society* or Tony Robbins in *I Am Not Your Guru*. You know you're with a being in this state when you start to become magical yourself. They're creating themselves, and it's infectious.

When a person is fully created, they're an opportunity for others to remember their true selves. It's as if they hold up a mirror of possibility. Ellen DeGeneres "came out," lost a network show, and inspired millions to embrace their identity. Marianne Williamson wrote mystical ideas into accessible words, and woke up a generation. Picasso saw the world anew, painted outrageous figures, and changed the art world forever. Whatever gift you hold, you are the only one who can bring it into the world. Don't you want to behold what that gift is, and share it with everyone else?

When I was a few months sober, I tried to end a terrible, tumultuous relationship, but I couldn't quite kick the guy. I knew he wasn't right for me, but I was addicted to that old pattern of staying in shit for all the wrong reasons. A couple weeks after a blowout fight with the guy at a gallery opening, I sat with my friend Kate at a restaurant on a Friday night on the Lower East Side. She was in a similar situation, so we sat for hours talking about how we shouldn't text our bad-for-us boyfriends.

Later that night, I walked down Second Avenue, holding my phone in my hand. I wanted to text him, but I also wanted to throw my phone down the sewer to stop me from doing it! I tried to pray, asking, "Okay, God, help me not to text him." A soft voice in my head said, "You're right. Don't do it." I stopped in the middle of the sidewalk, and shouted out loud, in front of a crowd of strangers, "Well, what do I get, then?" A bit dramatic, I know, but I needed to talk to my omnipotent invisible friend.

As if in a dream, I turned to the left, and saw my future husband—a man I'd crushed out on for a while—walking up the block. I turned back to the sky and said, "Wait, if I don't text this asshole, I get to be with *him*?" The voice spoke back to me and simply said, "Yes." I had stepped aside to behold myself, just for a moment, and the clearest vision of my future I'd ever seen appeared right before my eyes. Today, our relationship—totally real, perfect and imperfect—inspires clients and friends alike to know a healthy, happy coupling is available to anyone willing to "step aside" spiritually to make it happen.

Live Above the Law of Beholding

In order to start to live above the Law of Beholding, ask yourself, "If I could behold myself the way the universe does, what would I see?" It may just be the most beautiful sight you've ever witnessed: an open canvas, a space of pure possibility. Use meditation to behold yourself from this vantage point, seeing yourself not as a mind or body, but a space of unlimited potential. Start to get curious about what it would mean to live as a space of possibility, rather than a limited mind and body.

"If I could behold myself the way the universe does, what would I see?"

You're a blank canvas now, and as you create your life from this field of possibility going forward, the *way* you live will inspire others. Over time, as you create yourself anew, see the way others respond to

As you create yourself, you'll remind others of their own journey, and they'll start to see themselves in you and transform into *their* best selves in your presence.

the authenticity and greatness you generate from within. As you create yourself, you'll remind others of their own journey, and they'll start to see themselves in you and transform into *their* best selves in your presence. They'll also root and cheer you on in gratitude! It's a magical process.

Verification Point

After your morning meditation, light a candle, play beautiful music, and ask, "Who would you have me be? Show me what you want me to do. I don't know." Then, in your journal, write a letter to yourself from the universe, responding to your question. Write from your heart and intuition. Marvel at the response. As you write, you can listen to my music, too! My latest album, *The Lunar*, is specifically designed to create just such an awakened state. Go to Spotify or iTunes, search "Biet The Lunar," and enjoy!

42

THE LAW OF OPENING

You know how the Postal Service can't drop an oversized package into a house when the mail slot's too narrow? Well, I have some bad news. All too often, we live our lives with the same kind of limits on our ability to receive gifts the universe offers. When we limit our field of vision to a narrow opening, we play small, close ourselves off, and shrink the size of our "mail slot" so that it only receives the mundane and ordinary, never the brilliant or spectacular. Above the Law of Opening, though, we can use meditation to open ourselves up to tap and receive *all* that life has to offer.

Why would anyone consciously choose to receive only the narrow and small? Well first, the choice is unconscious, typically part of a long-standing pattern of behavior. Second, it's familiar. We're used to certain patterns, and it can be hard to let go of the comfort that we're used to, even if it's not what we really want.

To understand this law, consider an analogy. You drive a broken-down, used Toyota. Rusty paint, threadbare seats, barely runs. Your father, a man of means, offers you a sleek late-model Tesla, fresh off the lot. But you say, "I'm really attached to this old car. I'm used to it. I don't want a change right now. Thanks, though." Sounds absurd, but is it? In our lives, we're holding on to so many old ways of being that don't work—unhealthy relationships, jobs, or dietary choices, for starters.

Several years ago, I was making $1,500 a month as a DJ, caterer, and marketing assistant. In New York City, one of the most expensive cities on the planet! So, I shoplifted to, shall we say, supplement my income. I justified my theft with beliefs like "money is the root of all evil," or "big corporations are thieves anyway," and "they have a budget for theft anyway, no big deal." I'd grown up to believe that the pursuit of profit was unspiritual, that wealthy individuals were tainted by money, and those ideas weren't working out so well when it came to my bank account.

My bad habit bugged my boyfriend at the time, too. One day, he turned to me and asked, "Why don't we take a look at your finances?" He wasn't mean about it. He just wanted to help. You know what I did, though? I burst into tears, sobbing, and ran out of the room. I couldn't handle it. I held on to my narrow ideas about dollars so tightly I nearly had a nervous breakdown when anyone even mentioned money! At that moment, I'd hit rock bottom. I had to make a change, so I took my struggle into meditation.

Within a week, I manifested a (free!) money mentor as if from thin air. Right away, I started to work with him to grasp why I had gripped these beliefs so tightly. I realized I'd worried that if I opened my financial life to divine will, I'd be let down and disappointed. I wouldn't succeed, so why even try? In order to open myself to receive the gifts the universe intended for me, I realized I'd need to give up my own personal "used car"—shoplifting. So I buckled down, and asked to be open financially, and to let go of shoplifting. I asked a lot. As a substitute, I visualized receiving wealth in meditation.

As soon as I was freed of the habit, I felt lighter, and saw an immediate shift. For the first time, I made $2,000 in one month. A small start, sure. But the truth is, from that point I never looked back. That was the last month I ever made that little money, and my income has grown every month since then. Once I started to work with clients doing the work I do today, my income jumped exponentially. Though the opening was a bit painful—it involved more tears, to be sure—it led me to the life I live today.

Live Above the Law of Opening

In order to live above this law, you need to desire opening more than you fear failure. Realize that in many ways, the most powerful part of a meditative life is a cultivated ability to receive divine gifts. In this way, the hard work of opening is interior and spiritual, more than it is physical or mental. It is strenuous, though. A willingness to totally uproot belief systems and let go of old patterns is rare, to say the least. Rarer still is the willingness to sit in meditation for thirty minutes a day. But the value in opening closed channels to divine networks pays huge dividends.

> Realize that in many ways, the most powerful part of a meditative life is a cultivated ability to receive divine gifts.

So, observe where you're still holding on to beaten-down, used cars in your life. Conversely, where have you happily received your Teslas? For example, you may be open to love and blissed out in a happy relationship, but closed to receiving your dream career. Also, notice ways you block yourself via self-pity or vic-

"What blocks will I have to tear down in order to receive all I want?"

tim playing. Ask yourself, "What blocks will I have to tear down in order to receive all I want?" It may be anything from playing a martyr to procrastinating, as unique patterns present in all lives.

Verification Point

Observe an area of your life where, so far, you've been closed to receiving a gift the universe has in store. Then, incorporate this affirmation into your morning spiritual practice: "I am now worthy of receiving *all* the gifts the universe has to offer me, especially _____." Use the blank to specify an area in your life in need of opening. Use this affirmation for three weeks, and notice material changes or consciousness shifts.

43

THE LAW OF FOCUS

Like an Olympic skater focused on landing a triple axel. That's the level of focus you want to bring to bear on your aims. Easier said than done, though, right? All too often, we lose focus on our visions by paying too much attention to what our friends or professional peers are up to. If one of them succeeds in a vision you've long held, you may think, "Well, there goes that dream." Well, I have some good news for you. Above the Law of Focus, nothing could be further from the truth!

In that moment, though, you may feel distraught. It may almost feel like someone "stole" your vision from you. It's a common misconception. But your success is *yours*, specifically tailored to your unique gifts and talents. If someone next to you in life succeeds in a vision you've held, that was *their* potential they realized. It has zero to do with you. Nada. You have just the same capacity to realize that vision as you had before.

The thrust of this law is akin to the theologian Reinhold Niebuhr's famous prayer: "God, grant me the serenity to accept the things I cannot change, the courage to change the things I

can, and the wisdom to know the difference." The wisdom to accept what we *don't* have control over—the thoughts, words, and
actions of everyone else—comes via meditation and asking over
the long term. In terms of focus, this courage to change the things
we can is key. Our ability to make that change, though, requires
a tight line of sight on what we do control: our own thoughts,
words, and actions.

I recently heard an anecdote about Oprah that illustrates the
point. As a new talk show host early in her career, she competed
fiercely with much more prominent, established industry play-
ers. Reflecting on her career, she said that when producers and
agents asked her how she dealt with intense, competitive pressure for high ratings, she told them she was too focused on
what she was doing to have any mental space left over to think
about her competitors.

> Supersize your focus on what you can change so that there's no room left for anything else.

So, the Law of Focus is all
about the second phrase in this
prayer: the courage to change the things we can. One way to do
that is to supersize your focus on what you can change so that
there's no room left for anything else. Just as a scientist enlarges
the image of a tiny microbe under a microscope until it's all the
frame can fit, we can blow up the image of our aim so wide that
we can't even see all those things we can't change.

Recently, I worked with an artist who designed eyewear and
sunglasses. While she struggled to support herself, her super-
successful, high-net-worth girlfriend thrived. So she spent lots of
time thinking about the things her lover had that she did not, like
prosperity and professional happiness. Working through this law,
she started to see what a huge percentage of her thoughts were
out of focus.

I coached her to see that her plight in that very moment was the direct result of every choice she had ever made. But that was her good news! She had created the situation, yes. That also meant, though, that she could create her way out of it. Empowered, she started to focus on what she could control: her own life. As she drilled down on her aims, this focus expanded her sense of what she could accomplish.

Now the author of her results in life, she started to behold success, landing a line of sunglasses at Barneys. Her material success was just a by-product, though. Attentive focus to what she could control made her happier, and delivered a robust sense of self-worth and peace of mind. Unsurprisingly, these qualities also made her a better partner. She forgot her past obsession with her girlfriend's success altogether.

Live Above the Law of Focus

In order to live above this law, ask for the focus required to cease to compare yourself to others. Ask a lot. It's not an overnight task. Use meditative moments to pose open-ended questions: "Do I despair when others succeed in ways I want?" "Am I focused on my aims, or do I often focus on what others are doing?" No need to respond. In this case, questions matter more than answers. As you see yourself compare, note how it takes energy from creating the life of your dreams. You can't worry all the time, and have your dreams, too. Like my dear friend Peter says, "Are you a worrier or are you a warrior?"

> "Are you a worrier or are you a warrior?"

Another idea has always helped me with this law: you can't cherry-pick the perfect bits of someone's life without taking its flaws, too. Someone may have the career you want, but since they're human they also have lots of baggage you don't! Childhood traumas. Poor health. Who knows? We tend to focus on only the parts we'd like to have. Well, life doesn't work like that! Everyone has everything they need, inside and out, including you. So, remember this the next time you get into compare and despair. You'll bring yourself back to your own karma, which, may I remind you, is perfect!

Verification Point

In order to verify this law, get a sense for how often you compare yourself to others. An easy way to do this is to observe yourself as you scroll a social media feed. Notice the moment your thoughts drift to compare and despair. Then, split your attention to witness yourself. What do you see? You, scrolling a screen, trapped in negative thoughts. At moments like this, use a mantra to call your focus back: "You can relax." Say it several times. Notice how it calms. Good? Now, get off your ass and go focus on the life you want to create today!

44

THE LAW OF CRYSTALLIZATION

You thought I was going to talk about crystals, didn't you? Come on, admit it! Well, I'm not. When you crystallize a habit, practice, or belief, it melts into you so fully it's nearly impossible to shatter or alter. After thousands of hours of gratitude practice, for example, you can reach a takeoff point where a grateful mind-set propels itself. It's actually difficult to leave this state; it's fossilized in your being. When you crystallize a new practice, it typically takes a major shock to lead you back in the waters of an old one.

Once you've crystallized, you don't need a reminder to *be* that way again. When you crystallize, you become one with the state you seek. While it's possible to crystallize in a nanosecond via overwhelming white light spiritual experiences, for most of us the process entails the work of a lifetime. For instance, you used to have rage fits, but over time you crystallized in calmness. Where you once worried, trust and faith are now akin to automatic reflexes. In a sense, these traits have been encoded in your spiritual DNA. But you can't just crystallize on a cushion. It takes action.

Crystallization is a result of years of chipping away at the mold you're trapped in. On the way to see Michelangelo's famous sculpture the *David* at the Accademia Gallery in Florence, you pass through the Hall of the Prisoners, where you see four sculptures known as *The Slaves*. Part beautiful, muscly men, and part unfinished marble, these slaves represent the human struggle to free the spirit and reach our maximum potential. They also show that you can crystallize in a kind of mezzanine state before you've reached your highest possibility.

> In this sense, you are both the artist and the sculpture that emerges.

In a sense, you are both the artist and the sculpture that emerges. As you move to crystallize in a final, neutral state, you carve until you are fully realized. In this being state, no one can take crystallization from you. It's yours. Once you have made it all the way to being crystallized, there is no more fragility to your being. You fully remember yourself. In fact, a fully crystallized man looks like the *David*. No more carving to be done there! Above this law, you no longer live in a marble block prison of your own making.

Unfortunately, you can crystallize in negative states, as well. Humans trapped in these ways of being tend to be cynical, pessimistic, and argumentative. Obesity is a crystallized state that poses serious health risks. Addiction. Alcoholism. We can crystallize in gossip, worry, or rage as well. Stuck in these states, we may find ourselves confused as to why we can't seem to ever break free. When I was living as a junkie, crystallized

> When I was living as a junkie, crystallized in addiction, it was only my father's death that finally shocked me into pursuing sobriety, where the crystallized addict inside me could break open.

in addiction, it was only my father's death that finally shocked me into pursuing sobriety, where the crystallized addict inside me could break open.

So, crystallization can break, usually triggered by a shock of some kind. An avowed atheist has a near-death experience and finds God. A priest loses his faith and leaves the church. An addict hits bottom and gets sober. In these moments, a once fossilized state cracks open. In my own life, I've seen alcoholics crystallize as sober people in the clients I've helped guide to freedom. In certain cases, a series of strenuous, transformative exercises can shatter the old state and build a new one.

To put some color on the idea, let's use the film *Groundhog Day*. When we first meet Phil, a weatherman, he's crystallized in a cynical state. Entitled, arrogant, and ungrateful, he's a miserable guy. When he wakes up in a time loop, living the same day on repeat, he's so depressed that he eventually tries suicide. But when he falls in love, he starts to shift his daily ways. He learns to speak French, sculpt ice, and play the piano. Where before he was rude and caustic, he saves a child from an accident, gets coffee for his camera crew, and feeds the homeless. His fossilized state has cracked open. Once he's fully enmeshed in this new practice of loving-kindness, he wins the affection of the woman he loves and wakes up to a new day. He's crystallized in a new state.

Live Above the Law of Crystallization

Okay, so how do you crystallize a desired state? First, realize you get to decide what you crystallize in your life. Ask yourself, "What ways of being do I seek above all others? What lengths am I willing to go to in order to live in this state?" In your daily meditation, visualize yourself in a state you desire: filled with gratitude, living a risk-taking life filled with adventure, or in a perpetual state of generosity. The choice is yours.

Use the tool of asking to request the energy you need to crystallize. Remove yourself from or limit your exposure to people, places, and things that push down on your ability to reach a desired state. Surround yourself with others on similar quests or paths. Build or join communities with these people. Persist in taking actions every day, especially meditation, to reach your desired state or goal, *regardless of how you feel.*

Verification Point

You can crystallize any state you desire, but for this verification, we'll focus on gratitude. To begin to crystallize in gratitude, write a list of twenty-five unique, nonrepeating things you're grateful for every day in your journal for twenty-one days. You can read your lists aloud to friends or share them via email. You'll be amazed at how your worldview shifts.

YOU AND I, WE WROTE
THIS BOOK

It may sound a bit strange, but you and I, we wrote this book. So, thank you! "What are you talking about, Biet?" you may wonder. Well, let me explain. According to the spiritual work I teach, time runs in all directions. So, the future is actually the past, and vice versa. What this means, though, is that just as the past shapes the future, the future shapes the past. For example, kids' desire for a sweet, cold treat in the summer runs back through time, leading a man to invent ice cream decades earlier. Every woman who runs crimson red lipstick across her lips and feels sexy today inspires the creation of tube lipstick a century ago. Wild, right?

In *The Theory of Eternal Life*, Rodney Collin uses this idea to show how a great author like Shakespeare wrote his work fueled by the love and inspiration of his future readers. Collin writes, "all over the world, men are filled with noble, strange and tragic thoughts and feelings." As they read the Bard's work, they transfer their ideas and thoughts into the pages. As millions of readers do so, they make new the works they read, infusing them with feeling, passing back through time into the original manuscript.

This manuscript is at last found by Shakespeare. He sets
it on a table before him, turns over the pages, the words
run back into his pen, whose motion produces in him an
extraordinary fervor of power and understanding. When all
has run back, he is filled with ecstasy and knowledge. All the
millions of men and women have felt has entered into him;
the readers have created Shakespeare.

What a powerful idea. All the inspiration, ideas, and emotions
of his millions of readers traveled back through time to create
Shakespeare's timeless plays!

Just to be clear: I'm not Shakespeare! But in the same way
that time runs backwards to infect him with the inspiration of
millions, your yearning to awaken, your emotions as you read,
and your transformation as you work through these laws pass
back through time into my pen and out onto the page. So, thank
you! Thank you for dragging yourself out of bed to meditate in the
morning. Thank you for practicing asking, especially when you
didn't feel like it. Thank you for your willingness to be vulnerable
and open your heart and mind to the ideas in this little book. I
literally couldn't have done it without you.

As I've mentioned, this book is designed as a manual for living
life awake. I hope you'll return to it again and again, especially
when you feel stuck or need a bit of inspiration. As you live your
life, you'll change, but these laws never do! As you verify them
through the exercises I've laid out, you'll continually return to
an awakened state. I can tell you I overcame poverty, a junkie
mind-set, and tragicomic romances until I'm blue in the face, but
it won't matter until you verify the laws at play in your own life.
Once you've verified how you operate under and above these laws,
no one can ever take that wisdom from you. It's yours now, so go
out and use it to live your life in a way that inspires my next book!

ACKNOWLEDGMENTS

To Christophe, I honestly can't believe I found you. You are my whole life, my best friend, and my favorite part of reality.

For my Mama, I feel you with me since you died, and you are my mother, my sister, my daughter, my everything.

For Ula, my daughter, thank you for coming here just to die. I am ever grateful for your choice to live like a shooting star.

To my agent, Coleen O'Shea, thanks for believing in me and partnering with me. You are the best! It is such an honor to be a team with you!

To my editor, Zhena Muzyka, you inspire me every day. I love working with someone who is so alive and true to her mission on the planet.

To Libby McGuire, thank you for shepherding this little book to completion.

To Haley Weaver, you are the glue that holds it all together. This book wouldn't be here if it weren't for you.

The Genia Clan: Genia, thanks for always making me laugh and carrying such deep emotion in your eyes, you taught me what laughter is. I forgive you for ripping the head off my Hugga Bunch doll and throwing it out the window and filming it in slow motion. I would not have it any other way. Christine, Emma, Daniel, thanks for being the best Canadian family ever! Goga, always baby Goga to me. SeraGita, I love you so much. Alex and family, thanks for always keeping it real.

Family looks like . . . Dim, Julie, Michael, and Celeste, I don't care that we are not blood-related. To me, we are. Tanya, authentic, inspiring aunt and best friend to Papa Grisha, I love you. Rita, thanks for saving my life. Yuliya, Masha and Mira, and Magda thanks for helping Rita save my life once Papa died. Yelena and Dov, I feel so much love for you and am ever grateful to call you family. Olya and Kevin, la familia! Kathy and Steve Carroll for adopting me when I was a wayward artist. Terri Kosmicki, best mom-in-law ever! Franz, baby brother of my dreams, thanks for always keeping it champagne and caviar! Derv, thanks for being the best dad-in-law in the sky. Don, I guess you are my Godfather too now. I love you. The whole Koz clan, you mean the world to me. Lola, Tola, Raya, Misha, thank you for chasing me with borscht.

To Laura O'Reilly, you are the best friend anyone could ask for. Thanks for always being home to me.

To Paul Sado, thanks for always pushing and laughing, thanks for naming people Simkin in your movies. Thanks for telling me I was your Guru when I was still spinning records at Ward III.

To Ruby Warrington, my partner, my love, my sober curious genius. I love you. April 7th forever, baby!

For all the people who held me when I was running on empty and an active shooting star with no ground. Julia Van Riper, for being my best friend and always coming with me to the fifth dimension. Sergeo, east side to the west side, no diggitty.

Jacob Shak, brother for life. Sonia, thanks for showing me what presence feels like, tastes like, and smells like. Alisa, chocolates and gummies and horror films forever.

Max, you're a great film critic, I trust you implicitly. MT, soul friend. I do remember when we were cats in India and in some ways we will always be. Myles Mangino, thanks for giving me a couch when I was just a baby deer barely walking. Ben Carroll, all these years and we are still burning the poems and kissing the sky. Evan Krauss, thank you for always believing in me.

To Ran Cohen, my soul brother. I AM MAI. Glad we faced the terror of the situation together.

To Benmont Tench, thanks for believing in me all those years ago and allowing me to share my magic with you.

To Dr. Petrikovsky, thank you for saving my life, birthing Ula, and just being you.

Fellow oracles, we come back together again and again, just to forget. I am so grateful to have found you again. Caroline Murphy, you save my life all the time, and I really appreciate it! Peter and Lisa thank you for being alive! Sherri Brown, many, many lifetimes together, we got this! Thanks for helping me find my body! Lauren Zander, thanks for keeping it real, never letting me talk my way out of it, and for being a squirrel. Billy, you really are a dreams manifestation wizard. I'm so glad I created you! Michelle Murphy, if it weren't for that first time I met you, I would not be where I am today. I love you always, sister.

No one can get along without their girls! Tamara Edwards, I love you. I swear you are made of raw honey. Millana Snow, thanks for always keeping it astral. Sarah Perlis, you are a saint, I think. Casey Rotter, you are my most trusted sister and heart holder. Dana James, beauty is everywhere, thanks for helping me to always see it! Sara Reistad-Long, I will never forget how hard you have always believed in me and your ability to see my future. It is because of people like you that the world goes round. Andrea Praet, you're a doll, baby! Lauren Bille, inside us is the same magical stuff. I am so honored to see you over the years take out your magical inner perfection and wear it like a fucking crown. You inspire me.

Kyle, thank you. You are real and I see you and adore you and am so grateful for you every day.

To Katia, my blessing, my heart, my favorite person to hug and kiss.

For all the people who walk this road with me and do epic shit that inspires me as we ride! Jared Matthew Weiss, I see you and am always inspired by having such a dear friend like you. Shaman Durek, my brother, my homie, we are tied in the best of ways.

Jonathan Swerdlin, I don't know why but for some reason I feel like I have known you since the whole time thing was invented. Jason and Colleen Wachob, thanks for always paving a path of gold, you, we all! Charlie Knoles, thanks for being so doggone lovable, my friend. Elena Brower, I feel honored to walk this path with graceful warriors like you. Betty Kay Kendrick, gazing with you brings me back to where all things start and end. I love you. Miki Agrawal, thanks for disrupting her and being so real and authentic. I am honored to call you a sister and a friend. Andrew Horn, you are family. We are fucking alive! Radha Agrawal, you're a superpower heart, and you inspire me daily. You make my heart race. I love you so! Eli, you are a literal walking soul. Ebenezer Bond, you just get it and you make getting it super-simple. To me you are love. Jeff Scult: One. Golden. Thread. Jesse Israel, thanks for helping to make vulnerability and silence a thing the kids can get with. Taryn Toomey, Natalie Kuhn, and Jaycee Gossett, for being brilliantly alive and waking people up together. I really appreciate you. Nicole Centeno, alien baby: thanks for feeding me! Seth Cohen, I cried with you in the vineyard after we stood at the Syrian border. That is us, forever and always. Gemma and Sascha, there are very few people on this earth that I actually feel I am one with. I feel that way with you, though. Myk Likhov: Modern Om, baby; it's La'Russian mob style. Erin Claire, you are a light. I think you are made of light. Rachel Faith Tenenbaum, you are a kind and alive spirit. Whitney Kent Chamberlin, you are my magical friend and partner.

In no particular order, I could not have done this without you. Tyson Vogel, Sean Hoess, Karina Mackenzie, Rita Nakouzi, Dina Kaplan, Heather Matarazzo, Yisrael Campbell, Ryland Vallely, Lindsey Simcik, Krista Williams, Mel Nahas, Jo Blackwell-Preston, Laurie Daniel, Marc Lefton, Dr. Vincent Pedre, Chaya & Josh, Satya Twena, Justin Charles, Federica Baldan, Mark Krassner, Danny Steiner, Emily Fletcher, Allie Hoffman, Mukti, Basia, Michael Ventura, Brendan Fitzgerald, Jordan Younger, Elizabeth Kott, Kevin Feyen, Ashley Grace Allen, Elizabeth Cutler, Suzie Baleson, Noa Shaw, Iris and Lily and Gus, Carissa-Ann Santos, Nitika Chopra, Michelle & Ali, Bevin Butler, Annarita Aprea at Casa Angelina, Jenny Marcel, Jim Curtis, Alisa Leonard, Carolina Monnerat, Darrah Brustein, Brendan Doherty, Madelyn from Sedona, Liz Friedland, Lily Mandelbaum, Elisa Goodkind, Patrycja Slawuta, Sara Elise, Justin Daly, Kane Sarhan, Nick Kislinger, Matthew Makar, Erin Berman, Latham Thomas, Elliot Bisnow, Barbara Close, Sean Hanratty, Julie Anderson, Shira Abramowitz, Jeff Rosenthal, Jasmine and Paul Hawkins, Danielle Shine, Benjamin Shine, Jade Tailor, Ally Bogard, Waris Ahluwalia, Rosalie Lowe, Jess Coppinger, Geneen Roth, Sarah Beth Friedman, Jordan Younger, Gabby Bernstein, Jasmine Takanikos, Melissa Rosenfield, Paul Kuhn, Nikki Van Noy, Courtney Boyd Meyers, Donna D'Cruz & Tom Silverman, The Schusterman Foundation, Amy Taylor Smith & Craig Gallenstein, Moby, Joanna & Chris Jaouen. If your name is not here it's not because I don't thank my lucky stars for you every day; it's because my editor is screaming at me to stop. I love you. If you're a human who read this book, thank you. Please add your name here_____.

RESOURCES

Psychological Commentaries on the Teaching of Gurdjieff and Ouspensky by Maurice Nicoll

This six volume set changed my life. While I would not recommend reading or studying these books without a proper Fourth Way teacher or school, I would say that buying these books sometimes will attract such a school or teacher into your life. Ha! Who knows, that teacher may be me, as this work is rarely studied or practiced. I do, however, thank this particular philosophical system for being the backbone of all my understanding in reality. These books are heady, but they can take you into a trancelike state while you read them.

Tao Te Ching by Lao Tzu

Everything that can be said about enlightenment is said in this book. I made a joke once that since this book was written, it's hard for me to understand why any other spiritual book would ever need to be written! Of course I'm kidding, and I completely understand why, since all authors make a contribution. I use this book as a meditation, sitting with it in the times when I meditate daily. I also bring excerpts into meetings with my groups as I teach the Laws. So much insight from his words can be related to any of the 44 Laws. I recommend the translation by Stephen Mitchell, *Tao Te Ching: An Illustrated Journey.*

The New Man by Maurice Nicoll

The New Man is probably my favorite book ever written. It showed me exactly how the bible is actually a magical map to spiritual understanding, as Nicoll decodes its secret meanings. Life changing. Get ready to highlight the whole f-ing thing. I used to feel that biblical stories were confusing and unhelpful when interpreted literally, but Nicoll shows how the bible can actually be so wondrous and penetrable.

The Fourth Way by P. D. Ouspensky

Okay, I'm not gonna lie. If you get this book, you will likely find it as readable as a book written in hieroglyphics. It is really dense, rich, and almost impossible to understand. This book, like the first books on this list, is meant to be decoded by a real Fourth Way teacher (myself or someone else). I do, however, think this book can lead you to a school or to a proper teacher. It is good to meditate with and goes deeper into all the 44 Laws that my book is drawn from. If you wanna go deep and wacky, go Fourth Way with Ouspensky!

How to Get Out of Debt, Stay Out of Debt, and Live Prosperously by Jerrold Mundis

This book is the cat's meow for getting out of debt or learning how to make a buck. Mundis's work gave me the simple tools to understand and handle money, as well as practical tools from affirmations to spreadsheets. It helped me learn to earn! I highly recommend this book for anyone struggling with money, under-earning, or debt.

Self-Remembering by Robert Earl Burton

Robert Earl Burton teaches the term "self-remembering," which I use in this book. This book unpacks what divided attention is and more on self-remembering. Again, I would not recommend studying anything like this without a proper school or teacher, but if you want something to meditate with, this book is great. It also can lead you to open new doors of perception, as all spiritual texts tend to be a pathway.

Hero by Rhonda Byrne

This book is great for inspiration. It helps you feel like you really can do *anything*! I highly recommend it for raising your spirits and helping you remember who you truly are. Byrne helped me in knowing I was not alone in the world: people overcame hardship and rose to great success before me! This helped me know I too could do it.

The Power of Now by Eckhart Tolle

I'm not sure why I'm even mentioning this book, because if you read my book, you probably read this already. However, it's important I mention Eckhart Tolle because he is truly a modern example of truth and simplicity and wisdom. I feel like coming into his work will help you feel less alone and will open your heart to self-remembering. Before I had anything, or a clear idea of what I was doing on the planet, or a cent to my name, this book helped me to get into a higher state. I do believe it is when we are in higher states that the magical stuff happens.

Busting Loose from the Money Game by Robert Scheinfeld

This book is a treasure for getting out of the Matrix and starting to see the 4D world. It really helped me to see how not real the world is. With this book I was able to go into a real zone for flow state. I think Robert Scheinfeld is kind of out there, but everyone I have ever recommended this book to seemed to get similar results.

The Cloud of Unknowing by Anonymous

This book is all about that space you get to when you are climbing the mountain and you can't see below anymore and you can't see above. You are deep in a cloud. In this place you can't remember how far you have come, and you also can't really remember exactly where you are going. I found this book a solid meditation on how to commingle with that space of unknowing. Keep going anyhow and rise! I recommend the version in *The Cloud Of Unknowing with The Book of Privy Counsel: A New Translation* by Carmen Acevedo Butcher.

Steppenwolf by Hermann Hesse

This isn't the only work by Hermann Hesse that changed my life, since I've read all his books, but this text really showed me what it would look like if I could find my true self, find my real people, and transform reality.

The Complete Works of Florence Scovel Shinn by Florence Scovel Shinn

This book is basically Law of Attraction 101. I don't like too much airy-fairy crap, but this book is legit! I would not be where I am today without it. I read it, believed it, and followed all the concepts to a tee. If you are looking to attract major stuff into your life, this is a great handbook on how to do that.

Think and Grow Rich by Napoleon Hill

I always thought one day I would just become this superrich world-famous person. I never knew how or why, I just figured it would land on my lap. This book was one of the many wake-up calls that led me to see that I actually had to be a contributor to that occurrence. It gave me easy step-by-step guidance on exactly what was needed and what to do. I actually think this book is a must-read for all individuals. If you haven't read it yet, *run*—don't walk—and buy it and read it right away!

All Films by Andrei Tarkovsky

This man's films are meditations, and in watching them you will be transported into a state much like the one I live in every day now. When I was lost and searching, these films helped me as a compass to how I wanted life to feel and look, and the pace at which life should go once I was awakened. Beauty is the seed that sprouts the oak tree, and these films are the epicenter of beauty. In particular, I recommend three films: *Solaris*, *Andrei Rublev*, and *The Sacrifice*.

As I Was Moving Ahead Occasionally I Saw Brief Glimpses of Beauty, a film by Jonas Mekas

I found my initial states of presence while studying and watching avant-garde cinema. This work is a five-hour film that I watched at Anthology Film Archives in Manhattan, where I worked for a couple of years when I was eighteen years old. Jonas Mekas was a mentor to me and also a friend. "Worked" is a wacky word for what I did, because mainly I just drank wine and made strange music with Jonas, but this film changed my life. It reminded me of my life with my father and showed me how one communicates with life like a poem. This film is a huge puzzle piece of that state and a big breadcrumb on my long journey home to the divine.

ABOUT THE AUTHOR

Raised by an awakened shaman, Biet Simkin is a spiritual teacher and author who has practiced and studied the art of meditation for decades. Signed to Sony Records at the age of nineteen, she lived the rock 'n' roll glam life in New York City for years, until she fell to pieces as a heroin addict. In rapid succession, the tragic death of her infant child, followed by a fire that burned down her home, propelled her to get sober. As she moved from melt-downs to miracles, she began to teach meditation to rock stars, entrepreneurs, and CEOs, eventually founding the Center of the Cyclone meditation system and cofounding Club SÖDA, a sober curious quarterly event series.

Featured in *Vogue*, *Harper's Bazaar*, *Elle*, and numerous other publications, Biet has led mass meditations at the Museum of Modern Art in Manhattan and Sundance Film Festival, as well as luxury hotels from Los Angeles to the Amalfi Coast. In addition to creating in-room content for 1 Hotel, she has led workshops on how to meditate for executives from Sony, Lululemon, VICE, Adidas, and SoulCycle. Scoring these immersive experiences with original music, her meditations seamlessly weave stillness and a sexy rock 'n' roll edge into a one-of-a-kind experience. When she's not traveling, she resides in New York City with her husband, Christophe, and a fluffy Persian cat named Mukti.